NATURE
PROJECTS FOR YOUNG SCIENTISTS

PROJECTS FOR
YOUNG SCIENTISTS

NATURE

KENNETH G.
RAINIS

FRANKLIN WATTS
NEW YORK I LONDON I TORONTO I SYDNEY

Illustrations by Kenneth G. Rainis,
except page 100, by Stephanie Miller.

Photographs courtesy of:
Gervase Pevarnik, pp. 18, 20, 74; Bruce J. Russell,
BioMEDIA Associates: pp. 23, 45, 52, 56.

Library of Congress Cataloging-in-Publication Data

Rainis, Kenneth G.
Nature projects for young scientists / by Kenneth G. Rainis.
p.   cm. — (Projects for young scientists)
Bibliography: p.
Includes Index.
Summary: A collection of nature projects and experiments exploring
the five kingdoms of life, from bacteria to plants and animals.
ISBN 0-531-10789-2 (lib. bdg.)—ISBN 0-531-15135-2
1. Natural history—Experiments—Juvenile literature.
(1. Natural history—Experiments. 2. Experiments.) I. Title.
II. Series.
QH55.R35 1989
508—dc19   89-5662 CIP AC

ACKNOWLEDGMENTS

This book could not have become a reality without the loving support of my wife, Joan, and my children, Michael and Caroline.

Henry Rasof, my editor, persevered, and his critical comments and contributions helped make the book what it is.

Special thanks are due to colleagues Bill Kovar and Robert Iveson, who helped review the original manuscript and who encouraged me during the tough moments.

Many of the photographs in the book are by Bruce Russell, whose technical and aesthetic talents have added a special dimension to this work.

In memory of my father,
Vincent Rainis, my best friend
and a lover of books.

CONTENTS

NATURE
PROJECTS FOR YOUNG SCIENTISTS

1

BECOMING A
NATURE DETECTIVE

Nature can be viewed as a series of solutions to the problems of self-preservation and self-perpetuation. All life on earth must take in nourishment, adjust to its environment, defend itself against predators, and reproduce. The variety, complexity, and beauty of nature result from each life-form's unique solution to these tasks. The naturalist studies these solutions.

A naturalist often operates as a kind of nature detective. Like scientists and detectives, the naturalist uses the scientific method to probe and understand nature's secrets:

OBSERVE→GUESS→TEST→CONCLUDE

As a nature detective, you will work hard to **observe** what is happening around you, make a **guess** (a hypothesis) to explain what you observed, design a method (an experiment) to **test** your guess, and use your results (data) to **conclude** whether your guess was correct or whether it should be changed. Sometimes you will need to establish a control group against which to compare your results. A control group helps you determine whether your experimental results are valid.

Like all great naturalists, scientists, and detectives, you will find that your powers of observation will provide the springboard to your investigations. At times, your investigations will be aided by serendipity—the art of finding something valuable while you are looking for something else. Although everyone has these experiences, they are meaningless unless you can recognize their value. As the great scientist Louis Pasteur said, "Chance favors the prepared mind."

CLASSIFYING LIFE-FORMS

One of the greatest of all naturalists, Carl Linnaeus (1707–78), originated the concept of classifying living things in an orderly and scientific manner. His major work, *Systema Naturae*, is still used as a foundation for classifying organisms. We continue to identify organisms by a two-part Latin name consisting of the genus followed by the species. For example, *Acer saccharum* is the scientific name for the sugar maple.

Today, scientists recognize five groups of life, called *kingdoms*. This five-kingdom scheme includes monerans (bacteria), fungi, protists (algae and protozoa), plants, and animals. The chapters in this book are also divided in this fashion, going from bacteria, the simplest of organisms, to vertebrate animals, the most complex. An excellent guide to these kingdoms of life on earth is Margulis and Schwartz's *Five Kingdoms*, which contains valuable information for naturalists at all levels.

THE PROJECTS
IN THIS BOOK

The projects in this book are designed to help you learn more about nature and about yourself. Some of the projects are easy; some are difficult. Some are presented in step-by-step fashion, like a laboratory investigation, while others are simply ideas for you to develop.

You can work through the projects systematically to learn something about the different life-forms on earth, or you can choose one project that appeals to you. Either way, you will wind up with an experience that is enriching for its own sake, that may satisfy a class requirement, or that may be suitable for a science fair project.

Since classroom assignments and science fairs require careful methodology and formal presentation, you may need to do a lot of planning before you actually begin a project, and you will want to take careful notes as you go along. For example, even though your project may consist only in observing single-celled organisms, you will want to organize your findings in a coherent fashion so that it doesn't appear that all you have done is to make some random observations with your microscope.

For a valuable project that does not have to utilize all the steps of the scientific method, you could do a general investigation of microlife in a city pond and accompany your report with photographs of the pond, drawings of the organisms observed, and information about your sampling locations.

On the other hand, suppose you observe that bees are attracted to yellow flowers. You might want to prove that the color yellow attracts bees. You could conduct an experiment to test this hypothesis by preparing two identical paper models—one red; the other, yellow. You observe that a bee lands on the yellow flower. Have you proved your hypothesis? No, you have only gathered evidence (data) to support the hypothesis. There may be other variables, like flower shape or odor, that you have not investigated. You must conduct additional experiments that eliminate as many variables as possible before you have enough information to prove the hypothesis.

Both kinds of projects are legitimate and scientifically sound, and both have their place, but each will appeal to a different kind of naturalist/scientist. Science is the process of inquiry, one way of gaining knowledge about the world.

MICROSCOPES

You will need a microscope to do some of the projects in this book. For example, you will need a microscope when doing many projects with microorganisms. For other projects, a microscope would be nice to have. If you are studying butterflies, for instance, you may wish to examine them under a microscope to study their tiny scales. An excellent guide is Bleifeld's *Experimenting with a Microscope* (New York: Watts, 1988).

Building Your
Own Microscope

If you don't have access to a microscope, you can build your own "flea glass," which is adapted from a design by J. Cuff, a well-known eighteenth-century English microscope builder. (One of Cuff's clients, by the way, was the great Swedish naturalist Carl Linnaeus, who used a flea glass to aid him in classifying microlife forms.) This simple microscope works on the principle of magnification attained by a single convex lens. You use a sliding arm to adjust the focus. Depending on the curvature of the lens you use, you can achieve a magnification ability of between 10X and 20X—ten to twenty times the object's true size. You should be able to observe protists with sizes of 300μ* (0.012 inch) or larger, like *Paramecium* or *Volvox*. Building a flea glass is a worthwhile project in itself. Perhaps you can think of some useful modifications to improve its abilities.

To build your microscope, you will need the following materials and tools:

> hand or electric drill with ¾-, ¼-, and ¹⁄₁₆-inch bits
> 6 inches of 1-inch dowel
> white glue
> Velcro strip, ½ inch by 1 inch
> 2½ inches of ½-inch dowel
> 1½ inches of ¼-inch dowel
> 2 rubber bands
> canvas needle 2 inches long
> 20X pocket magnifier

To construct the flea glass, use the magnified view shown in Figure 1A as a guide.

1. Drill a ¾-inch hole through the 1-inch dowel about 2 inches from the end.

2. Glue a strip of Velcro to line this hole.

3. Use the rubber bands to attach the pocket magnifier to the drilled end of the 1-inch dowel.

4. Drill a ¼-inch-diameter hole ½ inch from one end of the ½-inch dowel. Drill the hole all the way through the dowel.

*μ is the symbol for micrometer. 1μ = 1/1,000,000 of a meter, or about 1/25,000 of an inch.

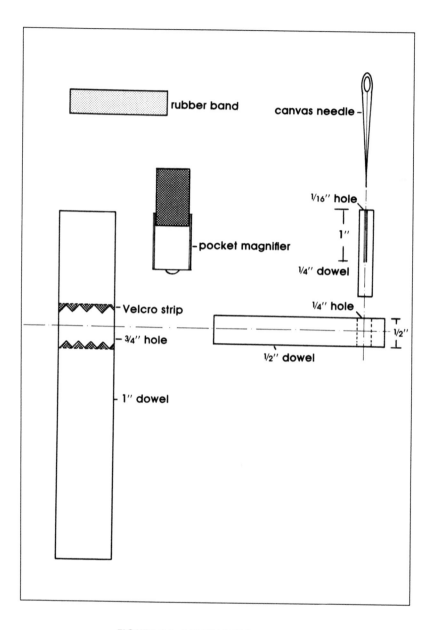

rubber band

canvas needle

pocket magnifier

$1/16''$ hole

$1''$

$1/4''$ dowel

Velcro strip

$3/4''$ hole

$1''$ dowel

$1/4''$ hole

$1/2''$

$1/2''$ dowel

FIGURE 1A. MAKING YOUR OWN FLEA
GLASS OR SINGLE-LENS MICROSCOPE

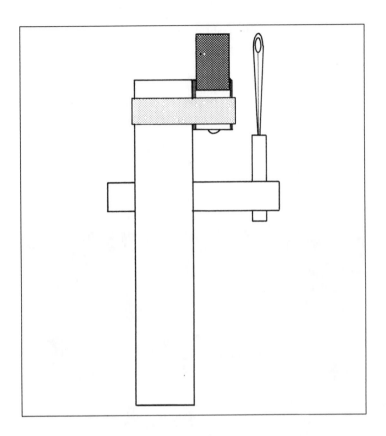

FIGURE 1B. THE ASSEMBLED FLEA GLASS

5. Drill a 1/16-inch hole in the face cut of one end of the 1/4-inch dowel and insert the canvas needle into this hole.

6. Insert the 1/4-inch dowel into the hole in the 1/2-inch dowel.

7. Insert the 1/2-inch dowel into the 1-inch dowel so that the assembly faces the side where the magnifier is attached.

Figure 1B is a drawing of the completed flea glass, and Figure 2 shows a photograph of the author's flea glass.

To use the glass, begin with a "point source" of illumination such as a table lamp—about 3 feet (1m) distant. Use window or open sunlight, or other light backgrounds for diffused lighting. **NEVER POINT THE LENS DIRECTLY TOWARD THE SUN. IT CAN DAMAGE YOUR EYES.**

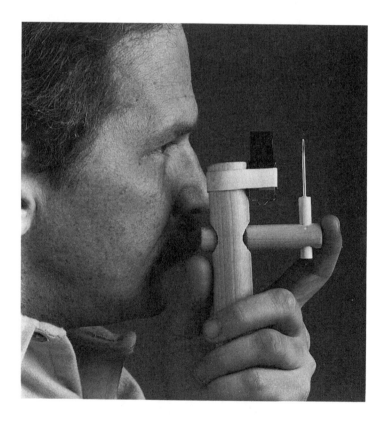

FIGURE 2. THE AUTHOR'S FLEA GLASS

To pick up water samples, remove the needle from the dowel and position it in line with the lens by manipulating the dowels. The friction fit of the Velcro should make the instrument easy to focus. See Figure 2.

You can adapt the microscope to hold other objects (flowers, insects, etc.) by using the sharp point of the needle. Simply reverse the needle in the hole of the ¼-inch dowel. See Figure 3B.

Microtechniques

When working with microscopes, the following techniques are especially useful:

Wet mount. The most versatile technique in microscopy is the wet mount. It will allow you to observe microlife under the microscope. Place a drop of water to be examined in the center of a glass microscope slide, then gently lower a coverslip (at a 45-degree angle) onto the drop.

Hanging-drop preparation. This is a drop of water that hangs vertically from the coverslip and allows you to view microlife forms enclosed inside it. The technique is useful in observing motile microlife forms. Use Figure 3 as a guide.

You will need glass concavity slides and coverslips, a toothpick, petroleum jelly, and tweezers. Use the toothpick to apply a thin layer of jelly around the cavity of the glass slide (Figure 4A). Place the drop of water to be examined in the middle of the coverslip (Figure 4B). Use the tweezers to quickly invert the coverslip so that the drop hangs (Figure 4C). Place the coverslip, with the hanging drop, over the cavity in the slide and gently press the coverslip to make a seal with the jelly (Figure 4D).

A

B

FIGURE 3. TO USE YOUR HOME-
MADE MICROSCOPE, YOU WILL
NEED TO KNOW (A) HOW TO
PICK UP A WATER SAMPLE AND
(B) HOW TO ADAPT IT TO HOLD
MACROSCOPIC OBJECTS.

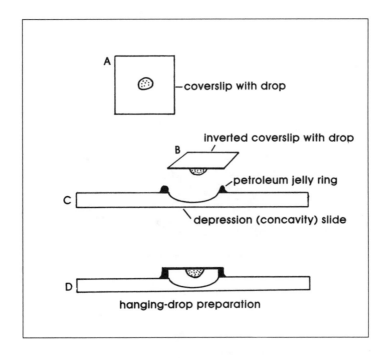

FIGURE 4. MAKING A HANGING-DROP PREPARATION

Dark-field microscopy. This allows you to easily view transparent microlife forms (for example, *Amoeba*) and very small forms such as bacteria. A special "dark-field light stop" is used to brightly illuminate the microorganisms while creating a black background that makes it easier to observe internal detail.

You will need a compound microscope that has a substage condenser. Your teacher probably has access to one. Simply cut out a circle of black construction paper, slightly smaller in diameter (about 7–9 mm) than the flat surface of the condenser lens (see Figure 4). Rack up the condenser lens until it is almost flush with the microscope stage. Use tweezers to place the paper disk in the center of the condenser lens (see Fig-

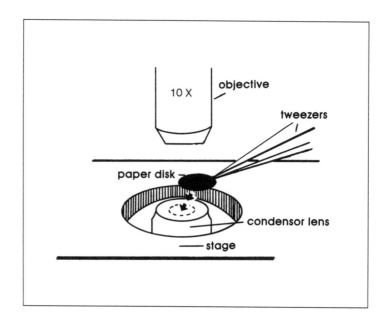

FIGURE 5. CONVERTING A BRIGHT-FIELD MICROSCOPE
TO DARK-FIELD ILLUMINATION

ure 5 for setup). Turn on the light source (or gather sunlight through the microscope's mirror), place a wet
mount on the stage, position the 40X objective, and,
as you look through the eyepiece, rack down the condenser until you see dark-field illumination similar to
that illustrated in Figure 6.

SAFETY—THE MOST IMPORTANT ASPECT OF ANY PROJECT

The most important ingredient for success is safety.

1. Be serious about science. A glib attitude can be
dangerous to you and to others.

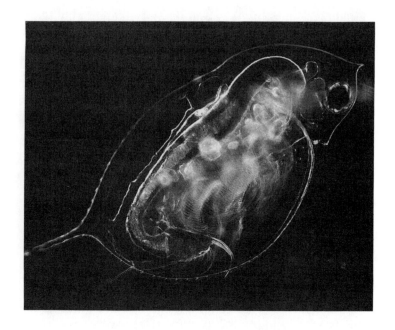

FIGURE 6. THE WATER FLEA, *DAPHNIA*,
VIEWED UNDER DARK-FIELD ILLUMINATION

2. Read instructions carefully before proceeding with any project outlined in this book. Discuss your experimental procedure with a knowledgeable adult before proceeding. A flaw in your design could produce an accident. **IF IN DOUBT, CHECK WITH A SCIENCE TEACHER OR A KNOWLEDGEABLE ADULT.**

3. Keep your work area clean and organized. Never eat or drink while conducting experiments.

4. Respect all life-forms. Never mishandle any vertebrate. Never perform any experiment on a vertebrate that will injure or harm the animal. Special guidelines must be followed when using vertebrates in science fairs.

5. Wear protective goggles when doing experiments involving chemicals or when performing any other experiment that could lead to eye injury.

6. Do not touch chemicals with your bare hands unless instructed to do so. Do not taste chemicals or chemical solutions. Do not inhale vapors or fumes from any chemical or chemical solution.

7. Clean up any chemical spill immediately. If you spill anything on your skin or clothing, rinse it off immediately with plenty of water. Then report what happened to a responsible adult.

8. Keep flammable liquids away from heat sources.

9. Always wash your hands after conducting experiments with any microorganism. Dispose of contaminated waste or articles properly.

Read More About It

Bleifeld, Maurice. *Experimenting with a Microscope*. New York: Watts, 1988.

Ford, Brian. *Single Lens*. New York: Harper & Row, 1985.

Headstrom, Richard. *Adventures with a Hand Lens*. New York: Dover, 1962.

Margulis, Lynn, and Karlene Schwartz. *Five Kingdoms: An Illustrated Guide to the Phyla of Life on Earth*. 2nd ed. New York: Freeman, 1988.

Winchester, A., and H. Jaques. *How to Know the Living Things*. Dubuque, Iowa: William C. Brown, 1981.

2

BACTERIA—
THEY'RE EVERYWHERE!

Bacteria, invisible to the naked eye except in large concentrations (called *colonies*), can be found in every environment on, in, and above the earth: within soil and ocean sediments; in the air; in and on plants and animals from fleas to elephants; and, of course, in and on human beings. Bacteria live on our skin, in our mouths, and in our intestines.

We tend to think that bacteria are only harmful, causing disease, discomfort, and sometimes death. Although some bacteria do cause all these things, most of the time we are not conscious of how bacteria affect our lives. For example, bacteria keep our skin clean and help us digest our food.

On a larger scale, bacteria are fundamental to the continued existence of life on earth. The number of environments (microhabitats) available to bacteria (and other microorganisms—fungi and protists) far surpasses those of plants and animals. Bacteria are uniquely adapted to exploit these habitats because of their small size and their ability to increase their own kind at phenomenal rates. Bacteria produce or process the major gases in our atmosphere (oxygen, nitrogen, and hydrogen), and feed on organic wastes and the remains of dead organisms. In this manner, bacteria are the major recyclers of the chemical components of life.

Although bacteria are very simple organisms, like the rest of life on earth they must compete and reproduce to survive. Most bacteria exist in three shapes—rods, spheres, and spirals. Another major group, the cyanobacteria (the blue-green algae) are much larger, many existing as long filaments, and colonies are visible to the naked eye. Almost everyone has observed cyanobacteria as the green, mosslike strands attached to rocks in brooks and streams. Some cyanobacteria, like *Spirulina* and *Anabaena*, are commercially raised for food and as a source of vitamins. Figure 7 shows a variety of bacteria types.

BECAUSE BACTERIA CAN CAUSE DISEASE, BE SURE TO WASH YOUR HANDS WITH SOAP AND HOT WATER AFTER EACH EXPERIMENTAL SESSION. POUR RUBBING ALCOHOL ON ANY CULTURE WHEN YOU ARE FINISHED TO KILL BACTERIA. DECONTAMINATE OTHER ARTICLES BY IMMERSING THEM IN RUBBING ALCOHOL FOR AT LEAST 30 MINUTES. PLACE DECONTAMINATED CULTURE MEDIA IN PLASTIC BAGS FOR DISPOSAL.

VIEWING THE SUBVISIBLE WORLD

Because most bacteria cannot be seen unless they are in large groups, you will have to provide a suitable microhabitat for them to grow and flourish. For example, boiled carrots are an excellent medium for *Bacillus megatherium*, a very large rod-shaped bacterium.

To make carrot media, cut carrot pieces and boil them for 20 minutes. Use boiled kitchen tongs to place

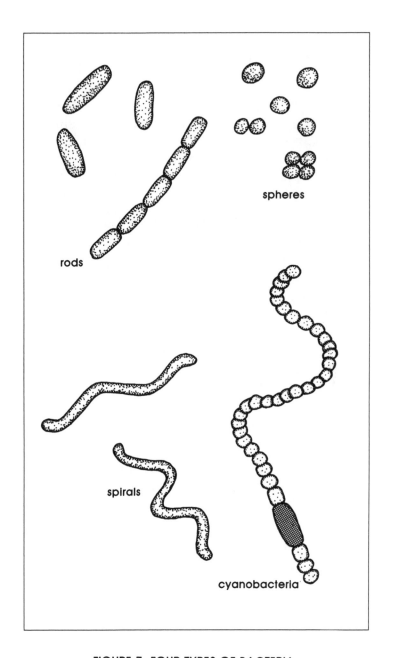

rods

spheres

spirals

cyanobacteria

FIGURE 7. FOUR TYPES OF BACTERIA

the boiled carrots (allowed to cool) on some dampened towels in a glass bowl. Cover the bowl with clear plastic food wrap. Let your culture incubate at room temperature for a few days in indirect light.

What kinds of growth do you see? Do colonies appear fuzzy, or wet and shiny? (The fuzzy growths are fungi.) From what you observe, do you have more than one type of bacteria colony?

• Use the carrot media technique to sample other bacteria growing on various surfaces, including countertops, plant leaves, books, and soil. Keep notes on the appearance and color of the colonies you isolate. Rub a cotton swab over the surface, then carefully swab the surface of the carrot to inoculate bacteria.

If you have a microscope, you can study individual bacteria cells from these colonies. To see individual bacteria cells, you will need to stain them on a microscope slide with crystal violet stain. Treat each slide as follows:

1.   Use a medicine dropper to add a drop of water to the center of the slide.

2.   Use the point of a toothpick to pick up a *very small* amount of material from a particular bacteria colony. Mix the material with the water drop on the slide to create a smear. Place the toothpick in a container of rubbing alcohol to decontaminate it before disposal.

3.   Allow the water drop to air-dry.

4.   Flood the smear with drops of crystal violet. Let stand 5 to 10 seconds.

5.   Gently rinse off the stain under a dripping faucet. Gently dry off the slide, except for the stained area.

6. Cover the stained area with a coverslip.

Observe the slide under a microscope at either 100X or 400X. *Bacillus megatherium* is a large rod-shaped organism that is easy to observe at 100X.

Draw what you observe. Can you observe spheres and spirals as well as rods? Make careful notes on the appearance of the colonies that the bacteria you stained came from.

• Try other culture media such as milk left open to air at room temperature, and boiled foods such as potatoes and apples. Does each of these media allow growth of the same microorganisms if not directly inoculated?

• Try swabbing water samples from ponds, puddles, and other sources onto carrot or potato media. Do you observe different bacteria colonies from those you observed before?

• If you have access to a microscope with an oil immersion objective, you can make a hanging-drop preparation to observe how bacteria move. See Chapter 1 for details.

NEIGHBORHOOD BACTERIA

Use the carrot (or other food) media technique to capture bacteria around your home and in your neighborhood.

• "Map" the bacteria in your home and neighborhood. Take photographs of bacteria cultures that grow out on carrot (or other) media. Do you find more bacteria on surfaces that have just been washed or after a rain? On surfaces that have been dry for a long time and then wetted? On soils that have been sprinkled on top of freshly prepared carrot media?

SOIL BACTERIA

Bury glass microscope slides at various depths in soil and mark their locations and depths with small stakes with labeled tags. After a few weeks, carefully dig them up, wrap them in facial tissue, and transport them back to your lab. Wipe off one side and stain them. Although most of the dirt particles will be washed off, there will still be plenty of bacteria to see! Observe stained slides under a microscope.

• If you do not have a microscope, you can make replica impressions by carefully pressing the soil-covered side of the microscope slide to the surface of carrot (or potato) media to transfer bacteria on the glass slide to the media. Be careful not to touch the media with any other surface.

• Bury slides in plant pots and then plant corn or other seeds on top or near them. Use a control. After a few weeks, carefully remove the slides from the growing root systems. Do you observe different bacteria populations on slides buried in pots with and without plants?

• Try burying slides in orchards during the fall. Bury slides just underneath the soil below trees and away from where fruits can fall. Do you notice any change in bacterial populations between the two slide groups? What do you suppose causes the change?

• Try the following technique on lawns. Examine buried slides both before and after application of fertilizer or pesticide.

BE SURE TO WASH YOUR HANDS WHEN HANDLING ANY SOIL THAT HAS COME INTO CONTACT WITH ANY CHEMICAL.

What changes do you observe? What effect does applying such chemicals have on the environment? How deep do these chemicals penetrate? How deep does salt applied to road surfaces penetrate soils and affect soil bacteria?

• Suspend microscope slides in pond or stream water. Stain the films created. Do you observe different types of microorganisms?

• Does drought affect bacterial growth?

• Do human activities have an effect on soil bacteria?

FOODS

Legend has it that yogurt and sour cream were discovered when ancient peoples tasted milk left out in the sun in hot Middle Eastern countries like Turkey and Syria.

• Make your own sour milk, yogurt, kefir (a kind of liquid yogurt), sour cream, or buttermilk. You can buy microorganism seed cultures or make your own. For example, a glass of milk left for 24 hours is an excellent trap for fermenting bacteria and fungi. Or you can make yogurt by adding a spoonful of commercial yogurt, one labeled as containing "active cultures," to a can of condensed milk. See if you can duplicate the conditions under which people in ancient cultures first might have discovered these foods.

DO NOT TASTE OR EAT ANY OF THESE FOODS UNLESS YOU ARE WORKING UNDER CLOSE SUPERVISION OF A SCIENCE TEACHER WHO SAYS IT'S OKAY.

• Why is buttermilk needed when baked goods are made with baking soda?

• Investigate acidophilus milk.

DECOMPOSITION

Collect decaying leaves, bits of bark, cut grass, pieces of moss, lichens, moldy fruit, suspect objects from your refrigerator, and so on, and study them for bacteria. Can you draw any conclusions about the presence of bacteria in or on these specimens?

• Bury microscope slides at various depths in a compost pile or in soil litter and sample for different bacterial populations.

THE TYNDALL EFFECT

In 1872, the English scientist John Tyndall observed that extremely small particles, invisible to the naked eye, could be made visible when a powerful beam of light was passed through air in a darkened room. You can use the Tyndall effect to observe bacterial growth without a microscope.

Fill a quart mason jar two-thirds full of water and add some pieces of dried dog food. Let the jar stand undisturbed for one or two days. What happens in the jar?

Fill another mason jar to the same mark with water. Place both jars in a darkened room and shine a flashlight at an angle on the side of the first jar. What do you see? Do the same with the second jar. Compare your observations. Now look at the contents of each jar using a hand lens.

Can you observe the Tyndall effect in a darkened room with slightly parted curtains?

Further Experiments

• Place hay or dried lawn clippings in two quart mason jars. Fill with water. Place the two jars in a 4-quart saucepan filled with about 2 quarts of boiling water and heat until the water in the mason jars boils for one minute. Allow the jars to cool; then put on the caps and tighten them. Label one jar Treatment #1 and the other Treatment #2. Set aside the mason jar labeled Treatment #1.

Observe both jars with a flashlight in a darkened room 24 hours later. Record your observations. Repeat heating the second jar (labeled Treatment #2) as before. Be sure to loosen the cap before reheating, then tighten afterward. In 24 hours, repeat the observations and reheat the jar (Treatment #2) yet a third time. In 24 hours, observe again.

What do you conclude from your experiments? Are bacteria killed by simply boiling foods or water once? Why or why not? Do some reading on Tyndallization and pasteurization. Are they the same or different?

• Do commercial products that advertise that they contain "billions of bacteria" for reducing septic tank problems really contain bacteria? Design an experiment to find out. If they do, how are the bacteria supplied, and how do they work? Try adding some oils (cooking oils and/or motor oil) to a mason jar containing a pinch of one of these products. Are the oils digested? What other commercial uses might there be? **DON'T FORGET TO WASH YOUR HANDS AFTER EACH SESSION OF EXPERIMENTATION.**

HEAVY METAL

Can trace amounts of heavy metals kill bacteria?

For this project, you will need to obtain prepared nutrient agar (in media tubes), sterile plastic petri dishes, and sterile cotton swab applicators. These are available from biological supply companies.

Be sure to follow the sterile technique instructions provided with your material. The success of your project is at stake.

Unscrew the media tube one-half turn and melt the agar in a water bath. After the agar has melted, allow the tube to cool in the water bath until it can be held in the hand. Carefully remove the sterile cotton swab applicator from its package and use it to pick up colonies of bacteria you collected on carrot media. Then dip the swab into the melted agar. Remove as much moisture as you can from the swab by rubbing it along the side of the tube before you remove it.

Pour half the contents into a sterile petri dish. Leave the other half in the water bath. Allow the agar poured into the dish to solidify. Clean three ½-inch (1- to 2-cm) metal disks (try copper, aluminum, and sheet metal disks) one at a time and place them on the agar as soon as they are cleaned.

1.   Wash the disks with soap and water.

2.   Place in a cup containing rubbing alcohol.

3.   Dip tweezers in the alcohol (to kill any bacteria on them) and remove the disks one at a time. Allow them to air-dry.

4.   Use tweezers to place each disk on top of the poured agar surface in the petri dish. Place the disks equidistant from one another in a circle, as shown in Figure 8.

Pour the remaining agar from the media tube on top of the disks. Allow the agar to solidify. Incubate the dish upside down for 48 hours at room temperature. Use a ruler to measure any "zones of inhibition" (clear areas without bacterial growth) that metal ions may have caused. Record your results. Some of the metal ions were leached out into the growth media. Did the metal ions react with the growing bacteria? Read about the toxicity of different metals.

• Use this procedure on other metals. Are some metals more toxic than others? Do you know why?
• Visit your local pharmacy and read the ingredients label of over-the-counter ointments and salves. Can you find heavy-metal compounds listed? Look for zinc, copper, and other metal element compounds.

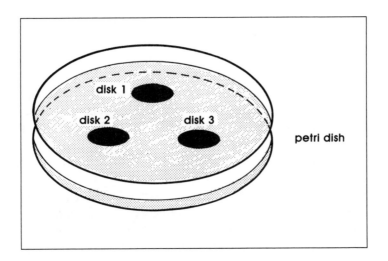

FIGURE 8. SETUP TO STUDY THE EFFECT
OF METAL IONS ON BACTERIA

Coat small, flat, plastic objects (such as tiddlywinks) with these commercial preparations. Do you observe similar results? Investigate other metals or compounds with this method.

IS PHOTOSYNTHESIS JUST FOR PLANTS?

Plants use light energy captured by the green pigment chlorophyll to produce food, a process called *photosynthesis*. Since oxygen is a by-product of photosynthesis, scientists can detect the presence of photosynthesis by measuring oxygen levels.

Hunt along the edges of streams and ponds for small bubbles, signs of oxygen production. Do you see any plants nearby? Is there anything that looks like algae? Look for blue-green strands attached to rocks or concrete. Collect some algae in a jar or test tube and take it back to your home or school lab. If you don't have access to a stream or pond, try to get some blue-green algae from a store that sells aquariums.

Separate the collected algae into two jars or test tubes along with collected water. Put one in the dark and one in the light. What happens after a day or so? Examine the algae under a microscope. Draw what you see. Would you be surprised to know that these organisms are bacteria and not plants? Do some reading on cyanobacteria—blue-green algae.

• Is it correct to define plants as organisms that photosynthesize? Should scientists reclassify plants as a form of bacteria? Do all bacteria photosynthesize?

• Experiment with different light colors and different temperatures on the photosynthesizing ability of cyanobacteria.

• Do cyanobacteria perform any useful function in aquariums, ponds, or streams?

• Find out whether cyanobacteria live in the ocean, in soil, on trees, or on stones in damp places. Then figure out why they do or do not live in these places.

• Do some reading on phosphate pollution. What does *biodegradable* mean? Check out the claims of manufacturers that their soaps are biodegradable.

A CLOSER LOOK AT
GARLIC AND OTHER POSSIBLE
ANTIBACTERIAL AGENTS

For centuries, people have believed that garlic has medicinal properties. For example, gravediggers burying victims of the plague in France in 1721 supposedly escaped infection by drinking a concoction of garlic and wine. Pasteur believed that garlic could kill bacteria. During both World Wars, garlic was used to prevent gangrene. Today, the same concoction used by the French gravediggers can be bought in French drugstores, garlic pills are sold in American health food stores, and magazines like *Prevention* periodically run articles on the wonders of garlic. Garlic also reputedly wards off vampires!

Does garlic have medicinal properties? You can answer this question by culturing bacteria using nutrient agar media plates (obtainable from biological supply companies), or bacteria collected on carrot or other food media.

You will be conducting "bacterial sensitivity disk" tests. Use a paper punch to punch ¼-inch (0.6-cm) paper disks out of construction paper. Use tweezers to dip the paper disks into various test solutions. Before you apply the disks to the agar surface, rub a cotton swab on the counter surface and then LIGHTLY rub it on the agar surface of a media plate. You can also use the swab to collect bacteria already isolated on your carrot (or other food) media. Crush garlic to extract its juice, or boil it. Use tweezers to dip paper disks in these liquids and to apply them (following drying) to the agar surface. Arrange the disks so that they are equidistant from one another on the media plate.

• Also test onions, leeks, shallots, turnips, lemons, and other fruits, vegetables, and spices. Find out which method of preparation is most effective: by grinding to extract juice, by boiling, or by other means.

• Test mouthwashes, cleansers, alcohol, and other substances for their antibacterial properties. Measure the zone of inhibition (the clear area around a disk) to determine which substance has leached out into the agar and is most effective. Compare your results to find the most effective substance or combination of substances.

• Food spoils easily in hot climates. Before the age of the refrigerator, people preserved their food by pickling it, drying it, salting it, and adding spices.

Experiment with these methods to determine why and how they work.

AFTER YOUR EXPERIMENTS, WASH YOUR HANDS WITH SOAP AND HOT WATER. POUR A SMALL AMOUNT OF RUBBING ALCOHOL ONTO AGAR PLATE SURFACES AND LEAVE AT LEAST 30 MINUTES BEFORE DISCARDING. BE SURE TO DECONTAMINATE ALL INSTRUMENTS AS WELL.

A CLOSER LOOK AT NITROGEN-FIXING BACTERIA

Some bacteria are specialists. Some generate methane gas, while others digest petroleum or secrete powerful toxins that cause illness. Still others, the nitrogen-fixing bacteria, convert atmospheric nitrogen into a form (ammonia) that can be used by plants. Other bacteria convert the ammonia into nitrites and nitrates, nutrients essential for growth. See Figure 9.

You can investigate these bacteria using clover, a common plant found along the roadside and in fields.

Carefully dig up the clover's root system and wash off the soil. Do you see any pea-size nodules on the roots?

Cut a small piece of nodule and crush it between two microscope slides. Separate the slides and stain using the crystal violet stain method described earlier. Under the microscope (at 100X; if possible, at 400X), you should observe pockets of rod-shaped bacteria in groups of four to eight cells inside a thin membrane.

Find out whether these bacteria indeed cause the nodules. Germinate clover seeds on damp paper towels. When they have developed a root system 1–2 inches (2–5 cm) long, place them in a shallow dish of water. Grind some clover nodules (15 to 30) and inoculate the young clover plants by mixing the ground nodule material in the seedlings' water. You are inocu-

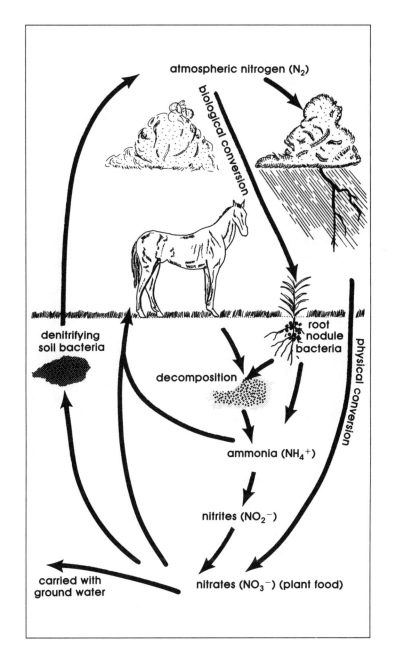

FIGURE 9. THE NITROGEN CYCLE

lating the young clover plants with nitrogen-fixing-bacteria contained in the nodules.

Use a control as well—young clover plants inoculated with pieces of a clover root nodule boiled for 30 minutes to kill any bacteria.

Wait a few days and then plant both groups of plants. After two to three months, dig them up and inspect for nodule formation.

What do you conclude about inoculating other clover plants using nodules? Which are the active ingredients: the nodules themselves or the bacteria inside?

• Read about leguminous plants. Can all plants incorporate nitrogen-fixing bacteria and form nodules?

• How are food crops inoculated with nitrogen-fixing bacteria? Will nodules left in the soil reinoculate next year's planted crop?

• Devise a method to inoculate crops.

• Does freezing affect the ability to inoculate clover plants?

MAGNETIC BACTERIA

In 1975, scientists discovered that magnetic fields affect some bacteria. Knowing this, you can perform some interesting experiments with very little equipment.

You will need to obtain some magnetotactic bacteria. Try the scientific supply companies. If you live near a swamp, marsh, river, or lake, you can collect and cultivate your own crop. To do the latter, obtain some bottom sediment from one of these locales (swamps are the best source). Fill a mayonnaise jar halfway with sediment and the rest with swamp water. Cover the sides of the jar with aluminum foil to reduce the growth of light-requiring microlife. Loosely screw on the lid and place the jar in a dark place for one to two months.

Once you have incubated your sediment, remove the aluminum foil and start experimenting.

• Use a bar magnet to attract magnetotactic bacteria. Try the north, then the south pole. Position one end of a magnet against the glass (where the water is, not the sediment) and hold it there for 15 to 30 minutes. Use a hand lens to determine if any bacteria congregate (white patch) in response to your magnet?

• How many bacteria can you concentrate using multiple bar magnets?

• Could you concentrate all the magnetotactic bacteria in your culture by wrapping a coil of wire around the jar to create an electromagnet using a battery?

• Try to concentrate bacteria close to the surface. Use a medicine dropper to withdraw some bacteria for closer study to see how they move and orient themselves using a microscope.

• Place a drop of CONCENTRATED magnetotactic bacteria on a microscope slide and add a coverslip. (More advanced researchers should prepare a hanging-drop preparation, and the microscope should be converted to dark-field illumination.) These bacteria are large and should be clearly visible at 100X magnification. Cut the light coming through the iris diaphragm so that the bacteria are visible. Sometimes adding a little India ink (dip a toothpick in some India ink and mix it with the water drop) will help you see bacterial movement. Bring a bar magnet close to the microscope slide and observe what happens. What is the orientation of these bacteria from your magnet? Do these bacteria line up in a certain direction? Do they have a north or south "pole"? Do the bacteria line up like iron filings?

- If you were in Australia and conducted this experiment, would you expect different results?
- Could you use magnetotactic bacteria to make a reliable compass?
- Do dead magnetotactic bacteria respond to a magnetic field?
- What happens if you divide a group of magnetotactic bacteria in half? Does one half repel or attract the other?
- How do you know if it's actually the bacteria that respond to the magnet and not the water?
- Experiment with other types of bacteria, as well as with different types of plant or protist cells. Do any of these respond to magnets? Try onion cells, leaves, flowers, protists from ponds or from hay infusions. Also experiment with buttermilk, yogurt, cheese, and yeast, all of which contain bacteria.
- Do chemicals affect magnetic properties?
- Does sunlight or oxygen affect magnetotactic bacteria?
- What purpose do you suppose the magnetic property serves? Design experiments to test your hypothesis.

Read More About It

Blakemore, R. P. "Magnetotactic Bacteria." *Science.* 190: 377–379, 1975.

_____, and R. B. Frankel. "Magnetic Migration and Bacteria." *Scientific American.* 245(6):58–65, 1981.

Bulloch, William. *The History of Bacteriology.* New York: Dover, 1979.

Dobell, Clifford. *Antony van Leeuwenhoek and His Little Animals.* New York: Dover, 1969.

de Kruif, Paul. *Microbe Hunters.* San Diego: Harcourt Brace, 1966.

3

FUNGI—THOSE
AMAZING SCAVENGERS

Fungi are the earth's scavengers. Along with bacteria, they perform an invaluable service, recycling organic material from dead life-forms. They do this by secreting digestive enzymes that break down organic material. Fungi are capable of digesting almost anything, as long as it is in a moist environment. .

You are probably familiar with mushrooms. But what you usually see and always eat is just the *reproductive* part of the fungus itself. The rest of the fungus lies hidden underground in the form of a netlike or cottonlike mass of slender, interwoven, hairlike tubes called *hyphae.*

Many fungi cause diseases, especially of plants. Gardeners and farmers constantly battle against molds, mildews, and rusts. Many other fungi form mutual relationships with plants, helping to provide recycled organic nutrients to their root systems. Others are used in baking breads and in making alcoholic beverages, and in industrial chemicals and medicines.

Fungi reproduce by means of microscopic reproductive bodies called *spores.* Each spore contains a single cell, protected by a thick wall and capable of withstanding temperature extremes for long periods without water. Fungi spores are incredibly light, so they are easily distributed by wind and air currents. Some can stay aloft for months!

BECAUSE MANY MUSHROOMS ARE POISONOUS, NEVER TASTE OR EAT ANY WILD MUSHROOM. DO NOT MAKE THE MISTAKE OF THINKING A MUSHROOM IS EDIBLE SIMPLY BECAUSE IT LOOKS LIKE A MUSHROOM YOU MIGHT FIND IN A SUPERMARKET. MANY EDIBLE MUSHROOMS HAVE POISONOUS LOOK-ALIKES.

STALKING THE WILD FUNGUS

Here are a few activities to better acquaint you with fungi.

• Carefully expose the shallow root hair systems of almost any wild plant and use a pocket lens to view them. Remove part of the plant's root system (be sure to include small clumps of soil) and place it on top of some black construction paper in strong light. You will see the tiny, transparent, hairlike threads of a fungus at work.

• Go mushroom hunting. Take along a penknife and a hand lens. Look for mushrooms in meadows, in dark moist places, on rotting logs, on lawns following a rain, or on compost heaps. Use the penknife to carefully move soil away from the mushroom's stalk (called the *stipe*) to expose the cottonlike mass called *mycelia* (see Figure 10). Place some mycelia along with soil in a plastic bag to prepare a wet mount in the labora-

FIGURE 10. MUSHROOM MYCELIA

tory to observe under a microscope. Adding a stain (methylene blue or a drop of fabric dye) will help you see individual hyphae clearly.

• You can also make mushroom spore prints, which are helpful in identifying mushrooms. After locating a mushroom having gills, cut off the stipe at the base of the cap and place it, gill side down, on a piece of white paper and cover the mushroom cap with a bowl for 4 to 6 hours. The spores will form a print on paper. To preserve the print, spray it with clear lacquer. Are spore prints different colors?

• Place a boiled seed (wheat, rice, or corn) in a small dish of water. Over the next week, you should see a mass of hyphae grow about the seed. Float bits of hyphae in a drop of water on a microscope slide. Try staining the hyphae. Do mold hyphae resemble mushroom hyphae?

• Explore your refrigerator, bread box, or other food storage areas for signs of fungal activity. Try to identify the fungi by using the Visual Guide to Fungi Types given later in this chapter. If you can't find any fungi, grow your own using moistened bread, citrus fruits, or leftovers placed in a sealed plastic bag. Be sure to get your parents' permission before doing this.

• Showers bring fungal spores. Attach a loop of sticky tape to a clean microscope slide. Hold it horizontally to capture the first few drops of a gentle rain. Later, use a microscope to examine the surface of the tape. Use Figure 11 as a guide in identifying the more common fungal spores.

• Design a project to investigate the presence of fungal spores in rain. How did they get there? Are they only in the first drops? If so, why?

PROBING A COMPOST PILE

You can investigate the mechanism of decomposition by using a compost pile. A compost pile is used to concentrate dead organic material, maximizing bacterial and fungal decomposition, to convert it into a form that can be used by plants.

Since the full decomposition process in a compost pile takes about six months, you may want to do this project for a science fair or as an ongoing classroom project.

If so, be sure to keep careful track of everything you observe and prepare a list of questions you want to answer.

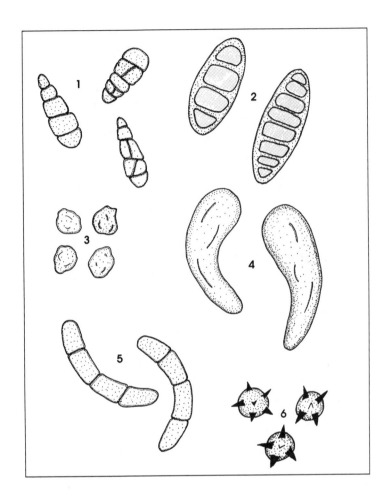

FIGURE 11. A GUIDE TO FUNGAL SPORES:
1. *ALTERNARIA*, WHICH CAUSES POTATO BLIGHT AND
BLACK ROT ON CARROTS; 2. *HELMINTHOSPORIUM*,
WHICH CAUSES OAT BLIGHT; 3. *PENICILLIUM*, THE
BLUE-GREEN FRUIT MOLD THAT IS THE SOURCE OF
PENICILLIN; 4. MUSHROOM SPORES; 5. *FUSARIUM*,
WHICH CAUSES YELLOW DISEASE OF CELERY; 6.
ASPERGILLUS, THE COMMON BLACK MOLD THAT
ATTACKS BREAD AND FRUIT (X 400)

To create a compost pile, build a small box in an appropriate place at your school, or away from the house if you plan to work at home. In the box, intermix layers of soil with leaves, grass clippings, sawdust, coffee grounds, and other organic material. Sprinkle water on the pile frequently. You should observe signs of decomposition within one to two weeks.

• Take notes twice a week. Do macro fungi (mushrooms and slime molds) spring up on the surface of the heap? What is happening to the plant material? Measure the pH of the pile using pH paper. Does the pH change over time or at various levels in the pile? Record the temperature. Also note any changes in color, smell, and height. What benefit does mixing soil have? Watering? What other material could be added to seed the pile with decomposers? Draw conclusions from your observations.

• Bury microscope slides at various levels and times in the pile. Use the method described in Chapter 2 to stain and observe any bacteria and fungi that grow. Do populations of bacteria or fungi change over time? Is such activity different in different parts of the pile?

• Look for natural compost piles in fields, woods, and vacant lots. Examine the leaf fall before and after winter if you live in a place where trees lose all their leaves. Does decomposition occur over winter? Does snow affect your compost pile?

• Use a soil test kit (available at garden centers) to test compost material. Do measurements vary within the pile? For example, is compost material good for all types of plants or only for plants that prefer acidic soil?

• Based on your observations, design a better compost pile. Would a sealed system work better than the open one described above?

THE SPOILERS
OF FOOD

Food-spoiling fungi have three main goals in life: (1) to convert their food into more of themselves, (2) to reproduce, and (3) to convert their food into chemicals that will discourage you or other organisms (including other fungi) from eating this food.

• Use the key in the next section to identify fungi responsible for food spoilage in your kitchen. Find out whether fungi prefer certain foods or whether certain fungi grow only on certain foods. Develop and test a hypothesis that explains your findings.

• Experiment with various foods to see whether any prevent spoilage or kill fungi. Try vinegar, onion or garlic juice, salt, hot pepper, lemon juice, and other foods. Develop your own powerful preserving agent to thwart aggressive fungi.

A VISUAL GUIDE
TO FUNGI TYPES

Here is a key you can use to identify fungi. You will need a hand lens or a microscope.

To use the key, begin with statement "1a" and proceed until the identification is certain.

NOTE: The spheres referred to below are *sporangia*, reproductive structures of certain fungi. They contain spores.

1a Examine your fungus. If there are fuzzy growth areas colored black, white, and/or gray,

GO TO 2

1b If there are fuzzy growth areas colored yellow or blue-green, **GO TO 4**

2a If, under a hand lens, the hyphae are not readily visible and there are numerous small spheres, the fungus is *Aspergillus flavus*.

2b If, under a hand lens, white to gray-colored hyphae are readily visible, **GO TO 3**

3a If the hyphae are beige-white and black spheres are not easily observed, the fungus is *Mucor*.

3b If the hyphae are gray to white and black spheres are easily observed, the fungus is *Rhizopus*.

4a If the hyphae are yellow with numerous dark spheres, the fungus is *Aspergillus niger*.

4b If the hyphae are blue-green to gray and few if any dark spheres are observed, the fungus is *Penicillium*.

PILOBOLUS:
THE SHOTGUN FUNGUS

Each morning at about ten o'clock in meadows, pastures, and barnyards the world over, a strange event takes place. *Pilobolus*, the shotgun fungus, shoots its small spore case into the air.

Pilobolus consists of a long, tapered stem supporting a bulbous body topped with a distinct black spore cap. The place where the stem and bulb join is reddish orange.

Pilobolus hurtles its spore cases onto blades of grass, which are eaten by horses, cows, and other grass eaters and redistributed in their dung. In this way, one *Pilobolus* colony can spread far beyond its borders. The fungus makes an audible "pop" when it shoots.

To investigate *Pilobolus*, you will need some of this amazing fungus. You can obtain it from biological supply companies, or if you live in a rural area, you can collect it on cow or horse dung.

• Once you have some actively growing *Pilobolus*, place it in the bottom of a mayonnaise jar. Place the cap loosely on top of the jar. Set the jar outside so that it will be in direct sunlight the following morning. Watch what happens.

Measure the firing angle of the fungus. Is there any connection between the firing angle and the angle of the sun at 10:00 A.M.? Can you trick the fungus into firing at a different time?

• Design a box with plastic windows to capture and study ejected spore cases. What holds them onto the plastic? Is this substance a good glue? Can you wash the cases off? (Simulate raindrops by dripping water from an eyedropper onto the plastic.) Study the spore cap with a hand lens. Create a model of it and practice "firing" it. Which end almost always comes into contact with the target surface? Can you think of a practical application for this design?

• Can you find any other fungi that reproduce the way *Pilobolus* does? Investigate other methods by which fungi reproduce.

THE LICHEN—
PROTIST OR FUNGUS?

A lichen is a unique "two-kind" organism—a fungus and protist living together in a mutually beneficial association. Figure 12 illustrates the three major lichen types, as well as some common forms found almost anywhere in the United States. An excellent reference source for identifying lichens is Hale's *How to Know the Lichens*.

fruticose lichen

crustose lichen

foliose lichen

FIGURE 12. COMMON LICHENS OF
THE THREE MAJOR LICHEN TYPES

• Use a razor blade to cut very thin slices from a lichen body. Use a magnifying glass to examine the general structure. Place one slice in a drop of water on a microscope slide. Use sewing needles to tease it apart. Place a coverslip over the teased material. Use a compound microscope to observe which part is fungus and which is protist. What benefit (if any) does each derive in the association? What color pigments can you observe in dried lichens?

• Do lichens normally found growing on tree bark occur growing on rocks, or vice versa?

• What conditions are ideal for lichen growth? How fast do they grow?

• Map lichen occurrence or heavy populations in your neighborhood or in a park, in a nearby forest or in other wild areas. Note lichen communities on a road map, topographic map, or other map. You can create your own lichen index to indicate quantitative data: for example, "5" for many lichens and "1" for very few. Use the lichen field guide to identify the lichens you encounter.

• Find out whether lichens are sensitive to air pollution, acid rain, fertilizers, or sulfur dioxide from power plant emissions. Do you find many lichens growing in cities or urban centers as opposed to locations away from these locales?

• Could lichens be used as pollution detectors? Use a map survey of lichen populations to aid in drawing your conclusions.

• Can lichens be boiled and the extracts used to dye cloth?

Read More About It

Hale, M. E. *How to Know the Lichens.* 2nd ed. Dubuque, Iowa: William C. Brown, 1979.

Large, E. C. *The Advance of the Fungi,* New York: Dover, 1962.

Lincoff, G. H. *The Audubon Society Field Guide to North American Mushrooms.* New York: Knopf, 1981.

Matossian, M. K. "Ergot and the Salem Witchcraft Affair." *American Scientist.* 70(4): 355–357, 1982. (Theory on how fungal poisons cause hallucinogenic effects in individuals.)

Miller, Orson, Jr. *Mushrooms of North America.* New York: Dutton, 1985.

Pramer, D., and N. Dondero. "Microscopic Traps." *Natural History.* 66(10):540, 1957.

Rolfe, R. T., and F. W. Rolfe. *The Romance of the Fungus World.* New York: Dover, 1974.

Sagan, Dorion, and Lynn Margulis. *Garden of Microbial Delights: A Practical Guide to the Subvisible World.* New York: Harcourt Brace Jovanovich, 1988.

4

ONE-CELLED ORGANISMS AND OTHER PROTISTS—INHABITANTS OF THE SUBVISIBLE WORLD

They live in pond water; on submerged rocks, aquarium glass, and bark; in soils and beach sands; even in snow. But you usually can't see them—except through a microscope. They are the protists, organisms usually consisting of one cell only and usually capable of moving. Some common freshwater protists are shown in Figure 13.

Although most protists are single cells, they engage in exactly the same life functions as other larger organisms: eating, making their own food, moving about, selecting partners for reproducing. Protists play varied roles in the microworlds they inhabit. Some are scavengers, feeding on dead remains; others feed on bacteria or hunt down other protists; still others make their own food the way plants do. Certain protists do a combination of all three.

Protists include the protozoa, algae, slime molds, and seaweeds.

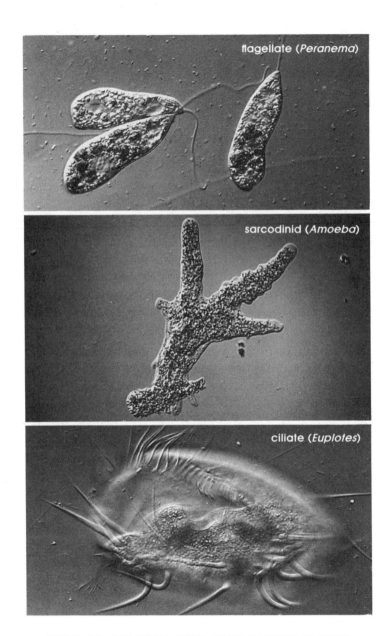

flagellate (*Peranema*)

sarcodinid (*Amoeba*)

ciliate (*Euplotes*)

FIGURE 13. COMMON TYPES OF FRESHWATER PROTISTS

A compound microscope is the best instrument to use for observing these interesting organisms, but a small single-lens microscope can also be used.

GREEN FILM

Protococcus can be found as a green film growing on almost any moist surface outdoors—trees, firewood, rocks, concrete. Mostly this green film has the appearance of a poor spray-paint job. You can probably find *Protococcus* in your backyard, in a local park, or in the woods.

• Scrape a little *Protococcus* into a plastic bag or vial and take it home or to school to observe under a microscope. Draw what you see. Your drawings, along with photographs and samples, could make an interesting project.

• Do you find *Protococcus* mostly on surfaces facing any particular direction? If you got lost in the woods, do you think you could orient yourself by noting the location of *Protococcus?* Record this information in your notebook. Also record the conditions in which you find *Protococcus* growing: light, moisture, temperature, type (tree, rock, and so on), and quality (smooth, rough, and so on) of surface. Your project could revolve around an assessment and description of your findings.

• What are the preferred growing conditions of *Protococcus?* If you have the time (it may take a year), design an experiment to test your hypothesis.

• Does *Protococcus* make its own food? Can you test your answer?

• Do other organisms inhabit the same habitat as *Protococcus?* Do other organisms inhabit *similar* habitats? Locate mushrooms, fungi on logs, mosses, and lichens. How do these organisms get food? Do animals and human beings have preferred habitats? Projects galore can be done observing various organisms in their habiitats.

SEAWEED:
MEDICINE OR MESS?

In the past, mariners believed that seaweed applied to a wound helped to stanch the flow of blood and to guard against infection. To test this notion, obtain some seaweed from the beach and carry it home wrapped in wet newspaper. Dry seaweed can be substituted. Seaweed can also be purchased from biological supply companies.

Collect bacteria from kitchen surfaces by using a cotton swab and lightly wipe the swab across the entire agar surface of five nutrient agar media plates. Close the lids after streaking. These will become the experimental "wounds" infected with bacteria. You will be observing the effect of various "treatments" applied to them.

Prepare the seaweed in one of two ways: (1) boil some seaweed for 20 minutes and allow the water to cool or (2) grind up some seaweed using a mortar and pestle and separate out the liquid formed.

Use a paper punch to make ¼-inch (0.6-cm) disks out of construction paper. Use tweezers to dip a paper disk into each prepared treatment solution. Allow any excess moisture to run off the disk. Place a disk from each treatment solution onto the center of two media plates.

Place an equivalent-size piece of wet and dry seaweed, respectively, onto the center of two media plates. Place a paper disk dipped in water in the middle of the fifth inoculated "wound" to serve as a control.

Figure 14 shows the experimental setup.

Open media plate lids only when streaking or placing disks on the agar surface—this will reduce contamination. Place media plates in an upside-down position in an area having a temperature of 75°F (25°C), away from direct light.

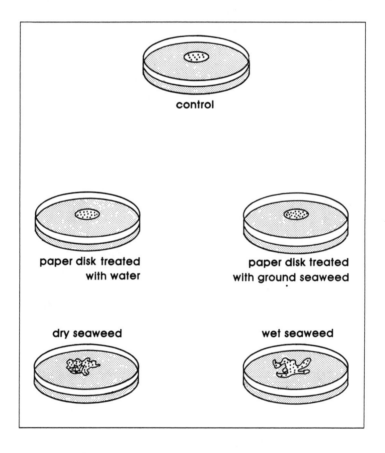

FIGURE 14. DIFFERENT SEAWEED PREPARATIONS BEING TESTED FOR ANTIBACTERIAL ACTIVITY

What do you observe about each treatment after two or three days' incubation? Does seaweed affect bacterial or fungal growth? Which treatment works best?

Try testing other solutions: mouthwashes, rubbing alcohol, disinfectants, cleaners. Do these chemical solutions show similar effects? Does the seaweed itself or a chemical it makes show antibacterial activity?

• Test small amounts of various soils or the fungus *Penicillium*, the green mold found in blue cheese and on citrus fruit, for antibacterial activity.

OUT OF THE OOZE

Early micronaturalists spent hours peering into single-lens microscopes, observing microlife in mud oozes, puddles, gutter sediments and waters, and other familiar locales. They then chronicled the changes they observed over time. For example, some micronaturalists observed that in winter or during dry periods many protists formed protective coverings called *cysts*.

To see what all the fuss was about, start by preparing your own protist cultures. Collect mud, dried grass clippings, gutter water and sediments, decaying leaves, and so on, put them into jars, and fill the jars about two-thirds full of bottled water. Let the jars stand several days in indirect sunlight.

Periodically remove water from the jars using an eyedropper, make wet mounts, and observe under the microscope. Use identification guides to try to identify what you see. Take careful notes on what you observe. Over time, try to follow the same organisms from the same parts of the jars. Try to identify the feeding strategies of different protists. For instance, where do the scavengers or the hunter-killers congregate in the jar? Design experiments to test for sensitivity to temperature, pH, light, gravity, magnetism, sound, movement, and other stimuli.

Here are some additional projects:

• Make a hanging-drop preparation to observe how protists move. See Chapter 1 for details.

• Try submerging pieces of sponge on a weighted line in a pond or similar location. After about a week, remove the sponges and thoroughly squeeze them into a collecting cup. Use an eyedropper to sample the cup and prepare wet mounts for observation with a microscope. What types of protists do you observe? Do these protist types change over time in, say, sponges immersed for a month or more? Why are sponges good protist traps? Can you devise other traps—for protists in soils, brook waters, or other locales?

• You may wish to study *Ichthyopthirius multifilis*, a parasitic protist that causes the Ich disease on fish. The Ich disease can be observed as tiny white spots on the fins and body of an infected fish.

As part of the life cycle of this organism, tiny swarmer cells burst from cysts located in the gravel in the aquarium and swim about, actively searching for a fish host. Find out when this swarming period occurs and whether it is affected by temperature, light, and so on. Then devise a method of killing the protist without also killing off the fish.

• Investigate other protists found in the gut of other animals. Make wet mounts of gut contents from termites, mealworms, cockroaches, and other insects.

• Using Figure 15 (A–D) as a guide, grasp the insect with tweezers (A), remove the gut (B), use teasing needles to tease apart the gut (C), and place a coverslip over the teased preparation (D).

ALWAYS WASH YOUR HANDS WITH SOAP AND HOT WATER AFTER HANDLING THE GUT CONTENTS FROM ANY ANIMAL.

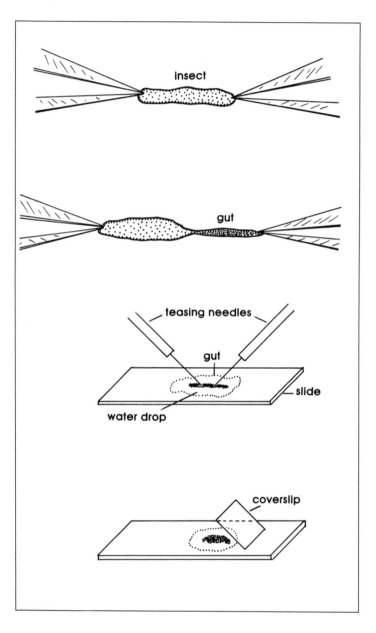

FIGURE 15. MAKING A WET MOUNT
TO STUDY INSECT PROTISTS

Read More About It

Dobell, Clifford. *Antony van Leeuwenhoek and His Little Animals.* New York: Dover, 1969.

Jahn, Theodore L., et. al. *How to Know the Protozoa.* 2nd ed. Dubuque, Iowa: William C. Brown, 1979.

Johnson, Gaylord, Maurice Bleifeld, and Joel Beller. *Hunting with a Microscope.* New York: Arco, 1980.

Needham, James G., and Paul R. Needham. *A Guide to the Study of Freshwater Biology.* San Francisco: Holden-Day, 1962.

Prescott, G. W. *How to Know the Freshwater Algae.* Dubuque, Iowa: William C. Brown, 1970.

Rainis, Kenneth, "Enteric Protozoa." *Carolina Tips.* Burlington, N.C.: Carolina Biological Supply Co., 1976.

Ward's Dichotomous Key to the Protozoa. Rochester, N.Y.: Ward's Natural Science Establishment, 1985. (Free)

5

PLANTS—
THE WORLD OF GREEN

From moss to towering redwoods, plants lend a refreshing green to much of the earth. They are the silent factories that transform the sun's energy, providing oxygen and food through a remarkable chemical process called *photosynthesis.*

All plants have a multitude of microscopic sacs containing the chemical chlorophyll inside their cells. It is chlorophyll—a substance that just happens to be green—that powers photosynthesis.

Plants are nature's pharmacy, having evolved hundreds of complex chemicals that play a vital role in their lives and in ours. Some plants are natural insecticides, and many are used as spices, cloth dyes, and medicines.

About half a million plants are known, and most are adapted to life on land. The plant kingdom includes all the familiar plants: mosses, ferns, shrubs, trees, vines, and herbaceous plants.

TESTING FOR
PHOTOSYNTHESIS

In addition to oxygen, one of the products of photosynthesis is starch, a food reserve. Since iodine applied to starch turns starch granules a deep blue-black, you can use it to find out whether a known plant has just been photosynthesizing, where it stores its food, or whether an unknown organism is a plant.

To apply the starch test, remove the green chlorophyll pigment that masks the starch. Boil the leaves (or other plant parts) for 5 minutes and place the boiled parts in a sealed container of rubbing alcohol for a day or so. Then transfer the plant parts to a tray containing Betadine, an iodine product available in drugstores.

BE SURE TO WEAR GOGGLES. IODINE IS POISONOUS, SO BE CAREFUL TO AVOID INGESTING OR SPLASHING YOUR EYES WITH THE BETADINE.

Allow this iodine-containing solution to react for 15 to 20 minutes. Gently wash off the iodine solution and inspect for the presence of starch.

First, try staining powdered starch (a control) to observe the color reaction.

Then do the following:

• Test leaves from trees, ferns, flowers, lichens, grasses, freshwater plants, and so on. Test leaves at various times of the day and night to see if you can detect different dark-brownish patterns indicating the presence of starch. Draw the patterns you observe. Does growing the plant in total darkness for three or four days make any difference? Test leaves that have mixed colors (like geraniums); and also test flowers (which are modified leaves). Make predictions about starch content before you do your testing. Are your predictions correct?

• Test roots and green stems. To prepare them, carefully use a single-edge razor blade or a potato peeler to make shavings of various plant roots or stems.

• Try testing different vegetables and fruits. Which ones have the most starch?

PLANT HOMES

Take field trips to various habitats and note how plants attract or are used by other creatures. Keep a habitat diary. Record what types of life-forms use different plants. Use photographs to illustrate your finds.

SURVEYING PLANTS

• Use field guides to identify as many plants as possible. Keep a notebook of your observations, along with drawings and habitat descriptions. Try to learn what environmental and physical factors influence plant type and design. For example, why are ferns not found in deserts and cacti not found in swamps? What special structural features allow cacti to prosper in dry climates?

• Make a permanent reference collection of plants from a given habitat. (Be sure to gather specimens only where collecting is permitted, and never take exotic or rare plants.) Dig up the entire plant, roots and all. Where plants are too big, take a small piece of bark and a twig with leaves. Place collected plants in a plastic bag to keep them fresh until you get home.

To preserve your plants, you will need a plant press. Use Figure 16 as a guide in making your own. (1) Bore about 20 holes in two pieces of 12 x 18 x ¼-inch plywood or use two pieces of pegboard instead (Figure 16A). (2) Place plants between sheets of newspa-

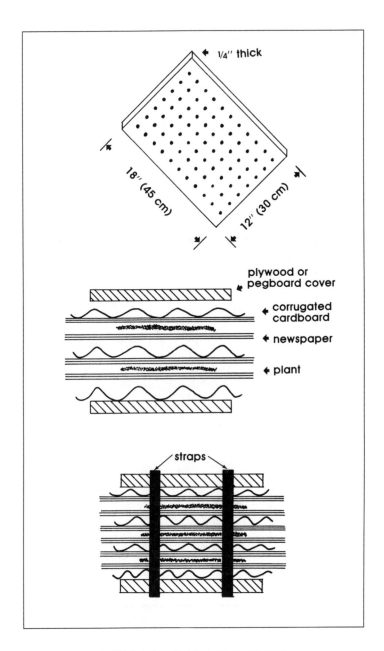

FIGURE 16. MAKING A PLANT PRESS.
THE FINISHED PRESS IS SHOWN IN C.

per, layer plant "sandwiches" with corrugated cardboard, and place them between plywood covers (Figure 16B). (3) Use straps or rope to press plants (Figure 16C).

Mount dried, pressed plants to heavy white sheets of paper (12 x 18 inches, or 30 x 45 cm) using small paper strips glued at each end. Figure 17 shows a whole mounted plant. Naturally, you may be pressing only the leaves. Label each sheet with the common

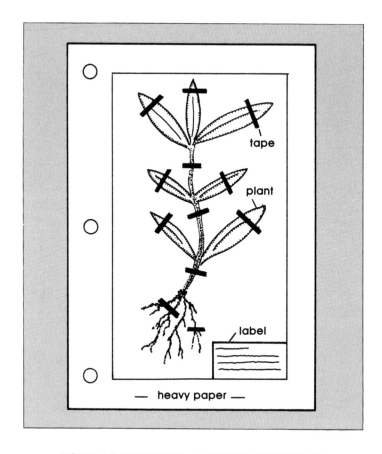

FIGURE 17. MOUNTING A BRANCH WITH LEAVES

and scientific name, date, and place collected, your name and the common features that place it in a particular group. Field guides will help you. Store your sheets flat in a cabinet or file box. Mothballs will help keep away insect pests that can damage your collection.

• Visit areas recently cleared of vegetation. Record which plants are initial colonizers. How did these plants get there? What adapts them to this role?

• Obtain permission to create your own nature trail in a park, wild area, or property. Either label plants in place or draw a map for others to follow. Try to point out as many plant adaptations as possible. Include information on seasonal changes.

PLANT DISEASES

Soots, mildews, rots, galls, and a host of other names describe plant maladies. Use popular garden books to identify diseases on plants near where you live. With your parents' permission, try to treat the disease(s) you find. Write a report chronicling how your treatment fared.

ROOTS

Roots anchor the plant and also absorb water and nutrients from the soil. Some roots also store food. Use the starch test to identify plants that have storage roots.

• What kinds of plants in your area have the longest roots? The biggest root systems? Don't dig up trees and bushes, but you could dig up weeds and grasses. Erosion may have exposed the roots of other plants. If you live near a stream, river, or pond, identify the plants living near or in the water and do some reading on their roots.

• Which plants would you expect to have the deepest or broadest root systems: plants that live in deserts or in tropical rain forests? Do some reading to check your answers. Perhaps what you learn will stimulate you to think of a project even if you can't make a field trip on your own.

STEMS

The plant stem not only holds up leaves and flowers but provides a vital transport system through which water and mineral nutrients move from roots to leaves, while food (sugar and starch) moves to the roots for storage.

• All stems have buds. A bud is a miniature shoot (a structure having a small stem and tiny leaves). Which is a stem—a potato or a sweet potato? Look for other examples.

• In winter, go out and collect twigs. Dry them out and use field guides to identify them. Label identified winter twigs by tying tags to them that list the common and scientific name, and the date and place collected.

• In most plants, water travels through tiny tubes that make up the *xylem.* Xylem in celery can be made visible by immersing a stalk into water colored by food coloring. After a few minutes, remove the stalk and observe the plant's tiny water pipes. Slice the stalk at various points along its length to trace individual tube bundles.

Investigate xylem further. Obtain some freshly cut white carnation flowers. Establish two study groups: one group with its stems recut at an angle about 1 inch (2-3cm) from the end, and the other not recut. Place both groups in vases containing water colored with food coloring. Time the passage of the colored water up the stems and to the flowers. Which study group had the faster water movement and the more

intense flower coloring? Investigate the effect of water temperature on dye movement.
- Do all stems carry out photosynthesis?

LEAVES

Leaves are the major photosynthesizing sites of plants. They have highly modified structures and their shape and arrangement are important clues in identifying plants.
- Start a leaf collection and organize it by leaf shape and arrangement.
- From your collection of leaves, what do you conclude is the best structural design to maximize photosynthesis?
- Observe the arrangement of leaves on any plant. What do you conclude about their placement on the stem?
- Notice how different plant leaves repel water. Do certain leaves have a fuzz (tiny hairs) on the tops of their leaves? Are leaf surfaces waxy, or sculptured to funnel water to or away from the plant? Use a spray bottle to mist leaves and observe the water droplets. How are leaf designs important to a plant?

USING PLANTS TO FORECAST THE WEATHER

Test these plant signs:

Impending thunderstorm:	Upturned leaves of silver maple trees
	Dandelions fold inward
Rain:	Dry grass in morning
Nice day:	Dew on grass in morning

Can you find other signs?

URBAN BOTANY

Conduct a plant inventory within a single city block in three different locations: residential, commercial, and industrial. Focus your attention on wild, not ornamental plants. What plants are common to each habitat? How do they adapt? Which habitat is more diverse—has the largest number of different plants? Collect and preserve interesting plant forms.

NEWTON'S APPLE

Does light affect plants in ways other than causing them to photosynthesize?

• Find out whether light affects color change when some apples ripen from green to yellow or red. First sterilize the apples for 2 minutes in a 5 percent bleach solution (1 part bleach mixed with 19 parts water) to prevent spoilage. **HANDLE THE BLEACH CAREFULLY.**
Wrap one apple in black paper to eliminate all light, and another in clear cellophane; wrap other apples in different colored cellophane. Wrap one apple in black paper that has little windows made of squares of clear and colored cellophane.

Expose the apples to light for several days. What do you find?

Try both ripe and unripe red apples (if available), as well as green and yellow apples. Experiment, too, with changing colors of cellophane on one apple, as well as with different types of light—sunlight, tungsten, and fluorescent.

• Experiment with other fruits and vegetables to determine whether light affects color or ripening.

• Does light affect root growth of vegetables such as potatoes, carrots, and beets? You will need a garden or good planters. As soon as the young plants emerge, spread different colored plastic sheets between rows. Make up a couple of hypotheses as to what will happen. After the growing season, harvest the plants and note the results. Were your guesses right?

• Find out whether light *color* also affects root size.

WEED CONTROL WITHOUT CHEMICALS

Is mowing the lawn the best way to control weeds? Design an experiment to answer this question and be sure to get your parents' permission before you begin. HINT: Try varying the depth of the cut.

WHO'S BEEN VISITING THIS FLOWER?

Some plants have flowers that consistently attract the same pollinators: insects, mammals, or just the wind. This helps ensure that pollen is transferred to a given flower of the same species.

For example, honeybees are attracted to flowers that are blue or yellow and have petals resembling landing platforms. The pansy is one example.

Make some observations of flowers. Note landing platforms, different odors (or no odor), night bloomers versus day bloomers, colors (or the lack thereof), shape, and so on.

Try to observe the pollinators. Wrap red cellophane over a flashlight to observe night pollinators without disturbing them. Construct your own "key to pollinators" and use it to make some general predictions about pollinators and flowers.

TREE RINGS

Have you ever counted the number of rings in a tree? Dendrochronology is the science of determining tree age according to the number of rings in the trunk.

Because of seasonal variations in cell growth in the woody parts of the trees, spring wood can be recognized as concentric light rings and summer wood as concentric dark rings. One set of light and dark rings, therefore, represents one year of growth.

Figure 18 shows a slab of red pine that is twenty-five years old. Growth was rapid during the first few years but slowed down between the fourth and sev-

FIGURE 18. TREE SLAB SHOWING GROWTH RINGS

enth years because less water (in the form of rainfall or snowmelt) was available for spring growth.

As the tree grew, crowding from nearby trees caused the rings to get progressively thinner. The shadows of early branches (arrows) can still be observed before they died off.

You can use this information to study tree growth near you. Try reading cut tree stumps or logs to reconstruct the age of the tree or the climate during the life of the tree. Check your findings against data from the weather bureau or from newspapers.

NATURE'S PALETTE

Is chlorophyll a single substance or a mixture of different substances? What about other plant pigments?

Chromatography ("color writing") is a technique that separates mixtures of substances into their components. You can use chromatography to separate and study various plant pigments.

Begin with a simple kitchen experiment to understand how this separation technique works. To simulate plant pigments, mix several drops of different food coloring dyes together in a small cup. Cut out a strip of paper towel 6 x ¾ inch (15 x 2 cm). Place a single drop of the dye mixture about 1 inch (2–3 cm) from one end of the strip. Allow the spot to dry.

Fill a glass with about 1 inch (2–3 cm) of water and position the paper strip so that it hangs in the center of the glass without touching the sides. Only the tip of the spotted end of the paper toweling should be touching the water. Use Figure 19 as a guide.

The water will rise on the paper toweling through capillary action. When it reaches the dye, it will continue rising with some of the dye. (Water dissolves the food coloring.) Notice how the different dye colors

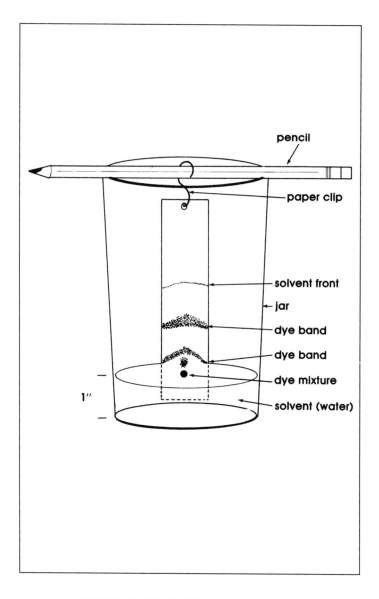

**FIGURE 19. SEPARATING DYE COLORS
USING CHROMATOGRAPHY**

separate out as the "solvent front" moves up the paper towel. The lighter pigments travel farthest upward on the paper towel; heavier pigments do not travel as far. The resulting image is called a *chromatogram*. A chromatogram is like a fingerprint, a visual representation of all the individual pigments present separated by molecular size. You can use it to learn about plant pigments and about plant processes that affect the pigments.

When you experiment with some plant pigments, you will need to use a different solvent from water. The best one is acetone, the main component in nail polish remover.

ACETONE IS EXTREMELY FLAMMABLE, SO AVOID OPEN FLAMES OR SPARKS. AVOID SKIN CONTACT OR SPLASHING MATERIAL IN YOUR EYES. WEAR SAFETY GOGGLES.

Making a Chromatogram
Use Figure 20 as a guide.

1. Select a green part to test.

2. Cut out a strip of Whatman #1 filter paper 6 x ¾ inches (15 x 2 cm) and make a point at one end of the paper.

3. Place a portion of the plant part about 1 inch (2–3 cm) from the tip of the point on the filter paper. Use the edge of a glass tumbler to roll and crush a THIN layer of the plant part onto the filter paper—the thinner, the better. Move another, intact area over the embedded area and make another impression.

Do this another time. This will embed as much plant tissue—along with plant pigments—as possible. The resulting paper strip should like Figure 20A.

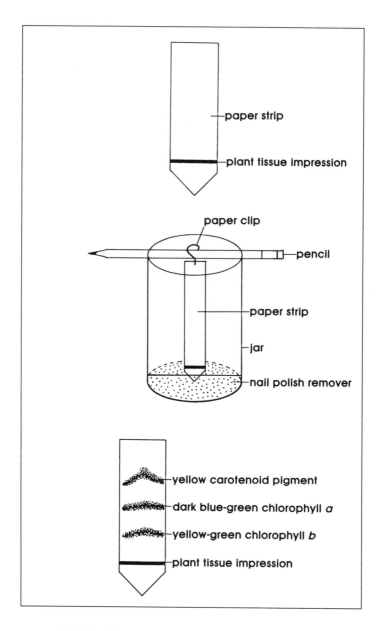

FIGURE 20. USING PAPER CHROMATOGRAPHY
TO SEPARATE PLANT PIGMENTS

4. Construct the setup shown in Figure 20B. Add about ½ inch (1.3 cm) of solvent, in this case nail polish remover (which contains acetone), to the jar. Position the paper strip so that just the tip touches the solvent. Make sure the paper is suspended in the middle of the jar, without touching the sides. Once you position the paper, don't move it.

Watch the solvent front move up the paper strip, meet the pigment spot, and transport the pigment mixture. After about half an hour, when the solvent front has reached almost the end of the paper, you should see distinct color bands; as shown in Figure 20C. The higher up on the paper a color band is, the smaller the pigment molecule.

Now you can answer the questions asked at the opening of this section—and others.

• Compare pigment fingerprints (chromatograms) of various plants and plant parts: plants kept in sunlight versus darkness, vegetables, fruits. Do chromatograms of carrots and other vegetables contain the same pigments as leaves? Use a potato peeler to make thin slices to press.

• Does season affect the chlorophyll content of leaves? In the fall, is photosynthesis still occurring?

• Certain plant pigments not involved in photosynthesis are soluble in water. Boil plant parts for 15 to 20 minutes to extract these pigments. Try cabbage, rose petals, beets, or other plant parts that are red, purple, or blue. Use a medicine dropper to "spot" pigment extracts onto filter paper about 1 inch (2–3 cm) from the tip of the paper.

Run chromatograms to see how many pigments there are in these plant types. Try adding drops of vinegar or baking soda dissolved in water to your extracts to see if you get a change in color. Read about pH. Does pH play a role in plant colors?

• Read about plant dyes. Can you make plant extracts that dye a small piece of cloth one or more colors? Will these dyes last or fade—by washing, or in sunlight?

USING A PLANT THERMOMETER

Rhododendron plants are adapted to conserving moisture by rolling up their leaves in both winter and summer. Observe a sprig of leaves from this plant (or a potted plant) at various temperatures and times of the year. Compare the amount of leaf curl to a temperature reading of a thermometer. Make your own plant thermometer chart and check to see how accurate it is.

AUTUMN LEAVES

If you did any of the projects on plant pigments, you will know that chlorophyll is the main pigment in leaves. But for a leaf to stay green, chlorophyll must be constantly synthesized.

• What in the environment actually triggers the cessation of photosynthesis? Is it something in the soil, the intensity of light, the length of the day or night, the temperature, or the humidity or amount or type of precipitation, or some other factor?

• Chart the color changes in the various trees and shrubs where you live, beginning in September. Keep track of types of vegetation, area, weather, and so on. It's probably best to pick a small section to keep your statistics manageable.

• Why don't leaves all turn the same color? Why do some leaves on a tree not turn at all?

• Why do some trees turn faster than others?

• Find out whether a dry growing season causes premature coloration. You will need to research rainfall and color display records in your area.

• Could mineral deficiencies affect coloration in houseplants or trees? Use a soil test kit to investigate this. You may be able to explain why one stand of trees in the park turns red and not another, or why one group of plants in your garden or indoor greenhouse is reddish. What minerals are involved, if any?

TROPISMS

Many plants actually move in response to certain environmental stimuli. Sensivity to gravity is *gravitropism*; to light, *phototropism*; to water, *hydrotropism*; and to touch, *haptotropism*.

• To investigate gravitropism, use corn seeds soaked in water for one or two days. Carefully arrange them in the bottom of a mayonnaise jar so that they are in a circle, equidistant, with their pointed ends facing inward. Use Figure 21 as a guide.

Carefully place a thin layer of nonabsorbent cotton over them. Fold white paper toweling to the approximate size of the jar opening and push it down into the jar to secure the seeds and cotton in position. Wet the paper toweling thoroughly and seal the jar with its cap.

Place the jar on its side and look at the four corn seeds through the bottom of the jar. Rotate the jar so that one kernel is pointing straight up. Use bits of clay to hold the jar in that position. Make sure the jar is placed in dim light conditions. Observe your experiment over 5 to 7 days. Make notes and draw what you see.

• Do different parts of the plant react to gravity differently? Do the roots and shoots always grow from

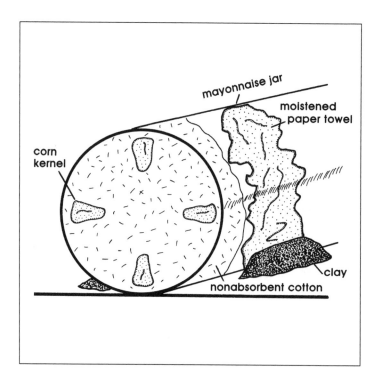

**FIGURE 21. INVESTIGATING THE EFFECT
OF GRAVITY ON SEED GROWTH**

the same part of the kernel? How long does a plant take to respond to gravity? Is it the same for all parts?

• Test potted plants (of the same type and height) for their response to gravity. Orient them in positions similar to those of the corn kernels—horizontal, vertical, upside down. Place all plants in the dark.

• Do plants react to the effects of circular motion? Do they react the same way as they do to gravity? Should astronauts on long trips take any special measures to counteract the lack of gravity in space?

• You can also use the Venus flytrap plant to investigate tropisms. Carefully investigate how the trap is sprung on mature plants. Do natural occurrences such as raindrops spring the trap? Do soil conditions affect the trap mechanism?

• Observe ivy and other vines for their response to touch. How do the growing tendrils react when they come into contact with solid objects? What happens if the tendrils are cut off?

• Hydrotropism can be observed when ground moisture is low. Construct a root observation box to observe this response. Use Figure 22 as a guide. Place dry and moist soil in the root observation box, as

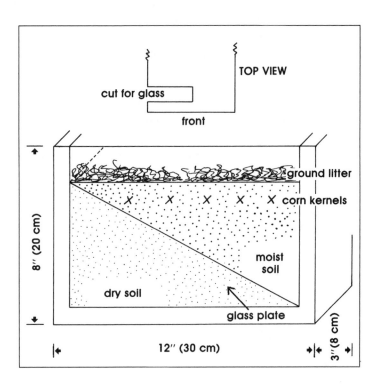

FIGURE 22. A ROOT OBSERVATION BOX

shown. Now plant five corn seeds along the glass plate about 1 inch (2–3 cm) deep. Cover the soil with mulch or grass clippings to hold in soil moisture. Draw what you observe over a two- to three-week period.

Do plant roots respond to soil moisture? If so, how? Do they seem to "search" for soil moisture? Try different types of soils—for example, clay, sand, and potting soil—and observe their moisture-holding capacities. Is a drenching rain more beneficial than a light, steady shower?

PLANTS WITH AN APPETITE!

"The most wonderful plant in the world." That's how Charles Darwin described the Venus flytrap plant after observing its unique sleight-of-hand. Of the world's 500 known types of carnivorous plants, only a few are found in the United States. It is best to purchase these from specialized growers or from biological supply companies instead of trying to locate them in the wild. As a group, they are remarkable organisms, with many rewards to be found in simply growing and observing them.

• Whatever plant you study (Venus flytrap, pitcher plant, or sundew), read about it and try to discern the strategy used to attract its catch.

• Use a camcorder with slow-motion capability to study these plants.

• Some insects (for example, ants) produce chemicals that are a defense against animal predators. Are these chemicals successful against carnivorous plants?

• Do these plants literally digest their meals—produce acids and digestive juices; do they "eat" their meal another way? You will need a microscope for this project.

PEST-AWAY

Test these natural plant-control measures for effectiveness:

ANTS
- Boiled cooled extract of elder leaves poured over nest.
- Marigolds planted near nests.

APHIDS
- Boiled extract of rhubarb sprayed on stems and leaves.

SLUGS
- Thyme (an herb) planted in a garden, or applied in dried form.

MOTHS
- Dry thyme and sage (herbs) in cloth packets.

FLIES
- Dried elder leaves in basket on a table.

**SEEDS—
CAPSULES OF LIFE**

Most plants reproduce by seeds. Their survival depends on their ability to reproduce. That, in turn, depends on mechanisms to disperse seeds. In flowering plants, seeds are protected by a structure called the *fruit*. In gymnosperms (pines and spruces), seeds are protected by cones. Ferns use spores to disperse themselves. (Look at the underside of fern leaves to observe spore packets.)

• Read more about seeds and fruits. Dry fruits, like green pea pods, do not contain the pulpy, fleshy material that characterizes fleshy fruits—apples, for example. Make a collection of seeds and fruits and record the fruit type, number of seeds, plant adaptations, and observed method of seed dispersal. Make a drawing of each seed you find. Use reference books to help identify plants and their seeds.

• Flight-test some of your collected seeds. Release each seed from a height and record how long it stays aloft and how far it travels. Do this on both windy and calm days. Diagram the flight path of each seed. Try counting the number of hairs on a dandelion seed. Is the number always the same? Try removing some hairs and see if the flight characteristics are still the same.

• Make models of maple, ash, or tree of heaven seeds. Use cardboard and pennies (for the seed part). How large a model can you build? Can you improve on nature's design?

• Investigate seed structure by dissecting various seeds (dried beans, for example). Sometimes it is helpful to soak the seeds in water for one or two days before dissecting. Use a drop of Betadine (available at drug stores) to test the seed for starch. Which structure does not stain?

• A seed planted and provided with the *proper* temperature and amount of oxygen and moisture will usually germinate. Does storage of seeds at freezing temperatures or very high temperatures (150°F, or 65°C) affect germination? What about alternating freezing and thawing? Will seeds germinate if placed between moist paper towels inside a sealed mayonnaise jar in which a small birthday candle has been burned to remove oxygen? Can you germinate seeds that are totally immersed in water?

IMPRESSIONS

In leaves, tiny pores called *stomata* allow the release of water vapor into the air, as well as the passage of gases (carbon dioxide and oxygen) into and from the plant during photosynthesis.

You can make impressions of these outer leaf surfaces to visualize these tiny stomates by using Duco cement. Use a brush to apply a thin layer of cement to the leaf's surface (above or below). After the cement dries, use tweezers to carefully peel away the resultant thin film from the leaf. Make permanent microscope slide preparations by placing the film on a microscope slide. Add one drop of corn syrup, and cover with a coverslip. Examine your slide under a microscope at 100X.

• How many stomates does a leaf have in an area 1 cm square? Is this number the same for a particular type of plant, or does it change.?

• Are stomates more numerous on the bottom or top surfaces of leaves?

• Could you use the number of stomates in leaves to identify different types of plants?

• Do desert plants like cacti have larger numbers of stomates than nondesert or tropical plants?

• Do plants keep stomates open longer in very wet conditions, or in periods of drought?

• When are stomate pores open on plant leaves? Closed? Relate your findings to the process of photosynthesis.

Read More About It

Beller, Joel. *Experimenting with Plants.* New York: Arco, 1985.

Hitch, C. J. "Dendrochronology and Serendipity." *American Scientist.* 70:300–305, 1982.

Knepp, T. *Beginning Botany.* Portland, Me.: J. Weston Welch, 1977.

Knutson, R. M. "Plants in Heat." *Natural History.* 88:42–47, 1979.

MacFarlane, Ruth B. *Collecting and Preserving Plants for Science and Pleasure.* New York: Arco, 1985.

Neiring, W. *The Audubon Society Field Guide to North American Wildflowers: Eastern Region.* New York: Knopf, 1979.

Peterson, L. *A Field Guide to Eastern Edible Wild Plants*. Boston: Houghton Mifflin, 1984.

Petrides, Lee Allen. *A Field Guide to Trees and Shrubs*. Boston: Houghton Mifflin, 1975.

Proctor, M., and P. Yeo. *The Pollination of Flowers*. New York: Taplinger, 1972.

Spellenberg, R. *The Audubon Society Field Guide to North American Wildflowers: Western Region*. New York: Knopf, 1979.

6

INVERTEBRATES—ANIMALS WITHOUT BACKBONES

Animals inhabit nearly every place on earth, from the bottom of the ocean to the tops of mountains. There are animals that crawl, swim, jump, and fly. There are big animals like elephants, and animals such as rotifers that are so small you need a microscope to see them. Animals are the most diverse form of life on earth. Recent estimates put the number of animal species at a hundred million or more, and it may surprise you to know that most of these species are insects. (There is, by contrast, only one species of human being!)

Despite the number of species, all animals can be (fairly) neatly divided into two main groups: those with an internal support structure (like a bony skeleton) and those without one. You and your cat have such a bony skeleton, but your pet sea anemone and starfish don't.

For a variety of reasons, invertebrates make the best subjects for animal projects. For one thing, there are more of them. For another, they are simpler.

Observing or working with their cells, organs, or genetic material is easier. And for another, they just don't "feel" the way many vertebrates do.

LOOKING AT HYDRA
AND OTHER MICROSCOPIC
ORGANISMS

How do you know when something is an animal? All animals share several features: they are motile; they have complex sensory organs; and they eat their food in some fashion. In other words, organisms that appear motionless can eventually be seen in some type of movement. And organisms that move aren't necessarily animals unless they satisfy the other two requirements. For example, a Venus flytrap moves to catch its prey but lacks complex sensory organs and doesn't really eat its food, even though it looks that way.

A good animal to begin experimenting with is the hydra. Hydras are soft, transparent animals that can stretch to nearly ½ inch (1–2 cm) when fully extended. Their tentacles make them appear to the eye like a frayed piece of string. In nature, they live in ponds and streams, where they attach themselves to plant stems and the undersides of leaves. The most common kinds are brown hydras and green hydras.

To collect hydras, obtain a large quantity of water plants or fallen leaves from pools, shallow lakes, or slow-moving streams. Place a group of plants with pond water or stream water in a white tray, and place the tray in a sunny but not hot indoor location. After about an hour, you should be able to observe hydras on the surface of the water and on the sides of the container. Use an eyedropper to transfer the hydras to a jar filled with pond water. If necessary, you can store the collected hydras in the refrigerator. Be sure to change the water weekly.

You might start by observing the feeding habits of the hydra. Transfer some of the hydras to a new jar filled with pond water and feed them newly hatched brine shrimp, bits of your dinner, or fish food. Do the hydras respond differently to different types of food?

Carefully use a fine needle to stimulate various parts of the hydra. Do this before and after cooling the hydra in jars in the refrigerator for 2 or 3 hours. Does temperature affect what you see?

• Study the effects of over-the-counter drugs such as caffeine and aspirin on hydra. Try different kinds of water—tap water, tap water that has sat in a jar for several days, bottled water, pond water.

• Obtain (from a scientific supply company) or try to collect other organisms, for example, daphnia, rotifers, and planaria. Try the same general types of experiments as you did with the hydra.

When you are through with your experiments, return the hydra where you found them.

INVERTEBRATES WITH CHEMICAL DEFENSES

Some invertebrates have nonlethal chemical defenses. Investigate the following organisms for chemical defenses: slugs, millipedes, and stinkbugs. Feed various insects to toads and frogs. What happens? Find out if other invertebrates use chemical defenses such as making themselves wet or creating a foul odor.

HATCHES

Most invertebrates reproduce by laying eggs. The eggs incubate for a while, then hatch. A lot of interesting experiments can be done to learn more about hatching.

A good animal to work with in the beginning is the brine shrimp. You can buy the eggs at pet stores. Follow the instructions on the cover for hatching and rearing brine shrimp; then strike out on your own.

Find out whether shrimp hatches are affected by water temperature. Can the eggs survive freezing and thawing? Experiment also with light, type of water, salinity, iodized versus noniodized salt, oxygen content, acidity, the presence of fertilizer or dirt, and the density of eggs.

• Find other invertebrates to work with.

CAUTION:
MOLLUSKS AT REST

After insects, mollusks are the most diverse group of animals on earth. Most mollusks have bodies that are covered by a shell. Typical mollusks are snails, slugs, clams, and oysters.

Since snails and slugs are so common throughout the United States, they are a good choice for projects. However, you may want to experiment with shellfish if you live near the ocean or an estuary. Shellfish (clams, for example) can also be found in lakes and rivers.

Catching land snails and slugs is best done on a drizzly night, early in the morning, following a heavy rain, or in generally wet places. Look for snails and slugs in the woods or gardens, under leaves, stones, and rotting logs. If you live in a big city, check the parks, neighbors' gardens, window boxes, and so on. You may be able to buy snails at some markets. You can track these mollusks by following their silvery mucus trails.

You can collect pond snails under pond weeds, floating plants, or submerged rocks. Saltwater snails and other mollusks can be found in tide pool areas, but be sure not to collect in protected areas. For example, tide pool collecting in many parts of California is generally against the law. (Of course, there's no law against touching and observing.)

Keep land snails and slugs in a sealed jar (with air holes) in the refrigerator (with your parents' permission). Keep aquatic snails in an aquarium or a jar with pond water.

• Crowd a bunch of snails (of either kind) together in a small space, like a plastic jar, so they cannot move. (Be sure to punch air holes in the top, or the snails will die.) Put the jar in the refrigerator (with your parents' permission). What happens? Keep some snails this way for several days, others for a week or two, and if you have the time, some for a month or more.

At various times, remove some snails from the jar and let them gradually warm up. Or place some of the snails in warm water for 10 to 60 minutes. What happens?

• Look for groups of snails or slugs in nature. Does their behavior resemble that of the snails or slugs in your "lab"? What do snails do during winter? When it's dry? When there's snow? Read about *estivation* in a book. Do snails and slugs estivate? What about clams, mussels, and oysters? Do some reading about commercial shellfish harvesting or talk to fishermen. Does what you find agree with what you have found out in your lab or in field investigations?

• Snails and slugs, of course, are famous for their slow pace. "Moving at a snail's pace" is one expression; "sluggish" is a word you probably have used or heard. Investigate how snails and slugs travel. Measure their speed. Is it that slow? Observe a snail's foot through a pane of glass. Do vinegar, baking soda, a solution, or other chemicals affect the foot or the snail's movement?

• What do snails and slugs eat? Are they scavengers? How do they locate food? Do they smell it? Do they use their tentacles to help them locate food? How would you find out? Find out why snails bred for the table are often fed mulberry leaves. Investigate the eating habits of other mollusks. How does an oyster eat, for example?

• How strong is a snail? How much weight can it pull? Will a snail pull only uphill? Do snails orient themselves according to gravity? Do they always travel headfirst uphill? Does a magnet have any effect on a snail's sense of direction? What are the effects of light and dark?

• People with gardens regard snails as horrible pests. Are there some plants that snails won't eat? Do some plants repel snails? Try marigolds and garlic. Some people put out beer in troughs to kill snails. Does this work? Can you design a garden that is snail-proof?

EARTHWORMS: NATURE'S SUBTERRANEAN ENGINEERS

Charles Darwin, the biologist who formulated the theory of evolution, made detailed observations of earthworms for years and believed they had some "degree of intelligence." He delighted in demonstrating earthworm behavior to houseguests. On his piano stood a row of flowerpots containing earthworms. At night, they would emerge to eat leaves. When certain low notes were played, the worms would retreat into their burrows.

Darwin reported that earthworms have food preferences. See if you can demonstrate this by building a worm box, adding soil and worms, and spreading different types of leaves on the surface. Also try fresh and dried grass clippings, flowers, and other plant parts.

Investigate worms in the field to see if they behave the same way in nature.

- Does sound or other vibrations affect your worms? Do your worms prefer rock to classical music? What good does it do worms to "hear"—if indeed they do?
- Are worms sensitive to different colors or intensities of light, amounts of moisture, temperatures, and surface textures? Experiment to see whether worms prefer one type of soil over another. If they do, can you isolate the "ingredient" responsible for the preference?

COLLECTING SOIL CRITTERS

A myriad of soil organisms can be observed by coaxing critters from the soil using a Berlese funnel. You will need a funnel, a large mayonnaise jar, a smaller glass jar, a small piece of insect screen, rubbing alcohol, and a gooseneck light. Refer to Figure 23.

Place the screen inside the funnel's spout. Add 1 ounce (30 ml) of alcohol to the small jar and place this jar in the mayonnaise jar. Place the funnel inside the opening of the large jar.

To use the Berlese funnel, place leaf litter and a small amount of the underlying soil, pine cones, and so on, into the funnel. Position the lamp 2 inches (5 cm) above the funnel, and turn on the light.

It may take a day or two for the light and heat from the bulb to drive the soil critters through the funnel into the collecting jar. Experiment with soils, leaf litter, twigs, cones, and so on, from different habitats. Use guidebooks to identify what you find.

You can use this collecting technique in projects of your own design to investigate insect diversity, the effects of pesticides in certain areas, the effects of pollution, and so on.

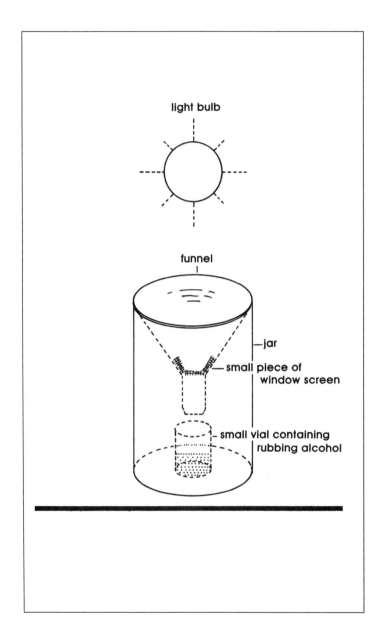

light bulb

funnel

jar

small piece of
window screen

small vial containing
rubbing alcohol

**FIGURE 23. A BERLESE FUNNEL APPARATUS
FOR COLLECTING SOIL CRITTERS**

THE PITFALL TRAP—
ANOTHER COLLECTING TOOL

The pitfall trap is another useful tool for the naturalist. It is used in projects to study invertebrate diversity, population densities, and distribution; and to compare samples from different habitats, explore seasonal or daily animal activity patterns, and to detect the effects of pollution or acid rain.

To install a pitfall trap, bury a large can so that its rim is level with the ground surface. Put a small cup at the bottom of the can and a wide-mouth funnel on top of the cup. Fill the cup with 1 inch (2.5 cm) of rubbing alcohol to kill and preserve what falls into the trap. Refer to Figure 24.

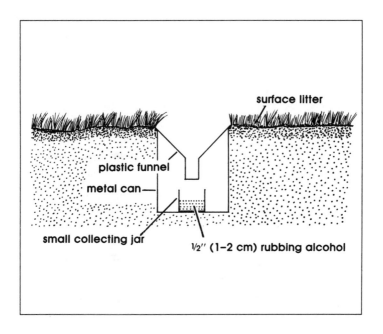

FIGURE 24. A PITFALL TRAP FOR
COLLECTING SMALL ANIMALS

To get comparisons, place your traps in different locations, or at different times of the day, or during different seasons.

A CLOSER LOOK AT INSECTS

• Investigate the effects on insects of light of different intensities and colors, of ultraviolet light and infrared, of gravity, of magnetic and electric fields, and of two light beams set at right angles to each other.

Work with insects in all stages of growth. Look for differences in responses at the different stages. Does species survival depend on any of these responses?

• Do some reading on pheromones and insect communication. Find out which insects, if any, communicate using their sense of smell.

• If you aren't allergic to bee stings, investigate the feeding behavior of honeybees. Can bees distinguish colors? How do they communicate? If you aren't sure whether you're allergic to bee stings, consult a knowledgeable adult before working around bees.

• Flyfishers tie artificial flies that they claim can fool trout. If you fish or know someone who does, do some checking to see if this is true.

• Try to create nonchemical insecticides or insect repellants using different colors of light (colored filters do the trick), magnetic fields, sound, various smells, and food derivatives (for example, lemon oil).

• Some scientists believe that ants (family Formicidae) contribute to the world's growing acid rain problem when they release formic acid defending themselves, communicating with one another, and dying. Formic acid makes up most of the acid in acid rain. Investigate the relationship between ants and acid rain. If such a relationship exists, how would you combat it—without using insecticides or creating a pollution problem?

SUGARING

Here is an easy way to attract moths and other insects for study without using expensive blacklight traps. Mix sugar with a little beer (under adult supervision) until you have a thick mixture. Apply the mixture with a brush to tree trunks at dusk. Return with a collecting jar and flashlight to collect the baited insects.

What types of insects are attracted to this kind of bait compared with a porch light?

Make a collection of insects captured this way. Refer to some of the books on insects in the reading list at the end of this chapter.

THOSE AMAZING SPIDERS

Spiders are everywhere. They live underwater in air-filled silk domes and hang from the cliffs of Mount Everest.

Spiders are easy to collect and work with. You can collect house spiders by holding a wide-mouth jar beneath them and slowly coming toward them from below. Most will fold their legs and fall into the jar. You can collect spiders in the field using a sweep net. Try weedy areas, or shake handfuls of leaf litter in a coarse sieve over a white sheet.

WARNING: DO NOT COLLECT WIDOW SPIDERS OR TARANTULAS. THEY ARE POISONOUS AND SOMETIMES EVEN DEADLY.

Figure 25 shows you how to recognize these spiders. Both black widows and northern widows are common throughout most of the United States, and tarantulas can be found in the Southwest.

Once you have collected some spiders, put them into a clear plastic box with small air holes. Feed them insects such as flies or crickets once a week, and keep a moist, quarter-size piece of cotton in a small dish in one corner.

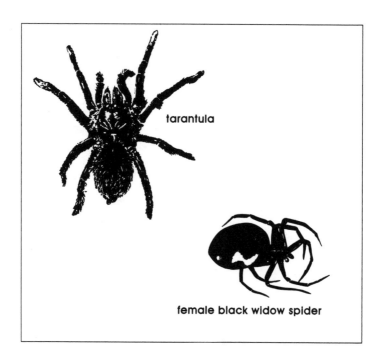

tarantula

female black widow spider

FIGURE 25. DANGEROUS SPIDERS
(DRAWINGS BY STEPHANIE MILLER)

Experiments with Silk

You probably have heard that spider silk is stronger than steel. Can you design an experiment to find out if this is true?

What is the silk made of? Does spider silk look the same as silk thread under the microscope? How do their qualities compare? How far can it stretch without breaking? How does this compare with thread or rope? How much weight will spider silk support before breaking? How much weight will a spider web support? Are different patterns stronger than others? What is the effect of moisture (or temperature, or light, or humidity) on spider silk?

Orb Weavers

Most spider webs—or nets—you will see are spun by a group of spiders called Araneids, which means orb weavers. The black and yellow garden spider is very common and a member of this clan. You can find these spiders in weedy fields and in gardens throughout the summer.

Collect some orb weavers if you haven't already. For each spider, build a spider net frame (see Figure 26) and put it in a spider cage or a blown-up clear plastic bag. Do your spiders weave nets? What time of the day do they start weaving? Observe the weaving process and try to draw the process in your notebook

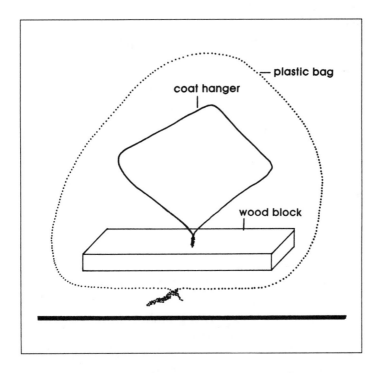

FIGURE 26. A NET FRAME FOR CATCHING SPIDERS

or on a piece of paper. Is the silk dry or wet when first spun?

Do your spiders build just one net, do they rebuild their nets, or do they build new ones? If the last is the case, how often is a new net built? Is the same net built each time?

Release flying insects in the cages or bags. Try using fruit flies, regular flies, or other small bugs. You can obtain fruit flies by leaving fruit outside a window.

Once you have observed normal web spinning, try some experiments to see if you can affect the spinning of the nets. Add coffee, aspirin, or other drugs in low concentrations to the water put in the cotton. Do the webs of drugged spiders look the same as normal webs?

Once you are through observing spiders, you may want to preserve some of the webs. The best way is to photograph them. Spray the web with white paint. Use black velvet for the background and light it from the side. If you don't have a camera, spray the web with white paint, then with a clear adhesive. Touch the web to the velvet while still tacky. Collect as many webs as you can.

Release the spiders when you are through with them.

SOWBUGS

If you have ever lifted up a rock or piece of rotting wood, you have probably come across the little animals called *sowbugs* or *pillbugs*. They roll into a ball when touched, you may remember.

Sowbugs are among the few land crustaceans—animals with two pairs of antennae that breathe using gills. Typical aquatic crustaceans are lobsters, crayfish, crabs, and barnacles.

Scientists believe that sowbugs have special humidity receptors on their antennae. To learn more about this interesting feature, collect some sowbugs in damp places around gardens, fields, or wooded areas. Check under logs or stones, or leave a piece of burlap undisturbed on the ground for several days.

Keep the sowbugs in a pan with dirt and covered with leaf litter and pieces of bark.

Now build a sowbug hygrometer. A hygrometer is a device that measures the humidity, or water content, of air. Build or buy a shallow, rectangular, opaque plastic box 9 inches (23 cm) wide, 12 inches (30 cm) long, and 4 inches (10 cm) high. Plastic food storage containers are good.

You now need to turn the cover into a piece of equipment that creates a different amount of humidity in different places. To do this, you will need the box's lid and some cotton.

Glue two long strips of cotton along the lid. Conduct a humidity test by wetting the cotton along half the lid's length. Place ten sowbugs in the middle of the box, close the cover, and wait about half an hour. Lift the cover and record the number of sowbugs in the low-humidity zone (unwetted cotton) and in the high-humidity zone (wet cotton). Repeat this experiment four or five times. Which zone is preferred? To be sure the bugs aren't rearranging themselves in response to some other property of the box, also run the experiment without wetting the cotton.

To see whether scientists are correct in asserting that the sowbug's antennae contain humidity receptors, use forceps to carefully remove the antennae from at least ten sowbugs. What happens when you perform the above experiment again? If the bugs still seem humidity sensitive, cover other parts of the sowbugs with petroleum jelly to shield them from the air. What happens now?

When you run the second group of experiments, be sure to include control bugs—bugs that haven't been operated on or greased up.

Do you better understand why sowbugs prefer damp places?

• Investigate other insects to see if they are humidity sensitive. Can you find animals that prefer dryness? Why would any animal prefer a lack of humidity?

Read More About It

The Brine Shrimp and How to Hatch Its Eggs. San Francisco: San Francisco Aquarium Society, California Academy of Sciences.

Goldstein, P., and J. Metzner. *Experiments with Microscopic Animals.* Garden City, N.Y.: Doubleday, 1971.

Headstrom, Richard. *Adventures with Insects.* New York: Dover, 1982.

How to Make an Insect Collection. Catalog No. 32W2196. Rochester, N.Y.: Ward's Natural Science Establishment, 1978.

Lawrence, Gale. *The Indoor Naturalist: Observing the World of Nature Inside Your Home.* New York: Prentice-Hall, 1986.

Milne, Lorus J., and Margery Milne. *The Audubon Society Field Guide to North American Insects and Spiders.* New York: Knopf, 1980.

Mitchell, John. *A Field Guide to Your Own Backyard.* New York: Norton, 1985.

Needham, James G., and Paul R. Needham. *A Guide to the Study of Freshwater Biology.* San Francisco: Holden-Day, 1962.

Rearing of Daphnia and Related Arthropods. Culture Leaflet No. 12. Rochester, N.Y.: Ward's Natural Science Establishment,

Reid, G. K. *Pond Life: A Guide to Common Plants and Animals of North American Ponds and Lakes.* New York: Golden Press, 1987.

Ruppert, E., and R. S. Fox. *Seashore Animals of the Southeast.* Columbia, S. C.: University of South Carolina Press, 1988.

Stokes, Donald, *A Guide to Observing Insect Lives.* Boston: Little, Brown, 1983.

Whitten, R. H. *Use, Care and Culture of Invertebrates in the Classroom.* Burlington, N.C.: Carolina Biological Supply Company, 1973.

Witt, P. N. "Spider Web-Building as an Example of an Innate Behavior Pattern." *Research Problems in Biology.* Series 2, 2nd ed. New York: Oxford University Press, 1976.

Zim, H. S., and C. Cottom. *Insects.* New York: Golden Press, 1987.

7

VERTEBRATES—ANIMALS
WITH BACKBONES

Think "animal," and one of a multitude of familiar images may appear: dog, cat, bird, frog, fish—yourself. Indeed, these are all animals, and although very different from one another, they all have something in common: They have an internal bony support structure called a *skeleton*. Animals without such a support structure are called invertebrates, animals without backbones. These organisms include insects, slugs, and worms. Some invertebrates—for example, shellfish—have external skeletons, or exoskeletons.

Vertebrates are but a small portion of the animal kingdom. What they lack in representative numbers they more than compensate for in complexity. All but a few have a brain and nerve cord. Their complexity and other attributes make them very adaptable, and verebrates occupy every type of habitat on earth. In short, vertebrates make excellent subjects of study.

Be sure to study the *Guiding Principles for Use of Animals in Elementary and Secondary Schools*, available from The Humane Society of the United States. You will be sure of properly treating vertebrates and other life-forms, and also of qualifying your project for a science fair. Science fairs usually have strict rules governing projects with vertebrates. You can obtain the guidelines by writing to the society at 2100 L Street NW, Washington, D.C. 20037.

BONES

You can learn a lot about vertebrates by studying their skeletons.

• Investigate the structure, shapes, and strength of bones from different animals. Which ones are solid? Which are hollow? Which are the strongest? Can you find a reason for the structure or shape of each bone? Does an overriding principle seem to be at work?

• Collect and compare examples of external skeletons of invertebrates (for example, clam shells) with skeletons of common eating fare such as chickens and cows. Which are strongest? Lightest? Can you make a generalization about structural differences between vertebrates and invertebrates with exoskeletons? Do you think the form (the shape) of the bones or shells is a result of their function? In other words, do certain bones have a certain shape so that they can serve a particular purpose?

"YOUR FEET'S TOO BIG"— OR ARE THEY?

Animals leave tracks. Knowing how to identify these tracks can tell you a great deal about the animal that made them.

1. Why can a bird walk on top of a snow drift or mud flat, when you or I would sink into it? Because the ratio

of the bird's weight to the size of its feet is less than the ratio of our weight to foot size. This ratio is called the sink factor. Sink factor is calculated using the following formula:

$$\frac{\text{weight (in kilograms)}}{\text{foot area (in square centimeters)}}$$

To calculate the sink factor of a snowshoe hare, for example, you would measure its prints and redraw them on graph paper as shown in Figure 27. Then you would find the number of square centimeters occupied by the prints. In this case the front feet are 20 square centimeters and the hind feet are 76 square centimeters for a total of 96 square centimeters. Since a snowshoe hare weighs 1.5 kg, the sink factor is

$$\frac{1.5 \text{ kg}}{96 \text{ cm}^2}$$

or 0.016

You can see that a much heavier animal will have a much larger sink factor. For example, an animal weighing 96 kg and with the same print sizes would have a sink factor of 1. Conversely, an animal that weighs less and has the same print size will have a much smaller sink factor. What size sink factor would an animal have with bigger feet and the same weight? Less weight?

"When measuring the combined area of an animal's footprints, you can either make a cast of the prints and measure the cast or simply measure the prints directly. Sometimes, as in snow, making a cast is difficult or impossible.

Make casts of animal tracks by pouring plaster of Paris into a suitable mold (a double-opened can or

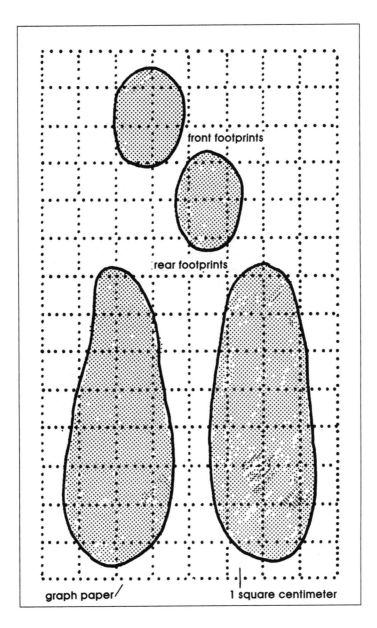

front footprints

rear footprints

graph paper

1 square centimeter

FIGURE 27. CALCULATING THE
"SINK FACTOR" OF A SNOWSHOE HARE

container) large enough to cover the footprint to a depth of 1 inch (2–3 cm). Wait 4 to 6 hours for the cast to dry. Apply ink to the cast and use it as a stamp to make an impression on graph paper as an aid in taking Sink Factor measurements.

You can do some of the following projects using books or working in the field:

• Calculate your own Sink Factor with and without wearing skis, snowshoes, or diving fins. Do these adaptations make a difference?

• Study different birds, especially shore and aquatic birds. What adaptations (if any) help birds reduce their Sink Factor?

• Use guides to predict which animals are best adapted to snow. If possible, do fieldwork to test your prediction. Are snowshoe hares really better adapted to snow than other rabbits?

• When you find tracks, try to identify the animal that made them and figure out if the animal was running or walking, whether it has claws or hooves, whether it was digging or pawing. Are there lots of one type of animal in the area? Can you find any killing sites, with feathers, blood, and signs of a fight?

BIRD MIGRATION

Every winter, when temperatures drop in northern latitudes, billions of birds migrate south to warmer climates. And every spring, when temperatures rise up north, these same birds fly north to their breeding grounds, sometimes returning to within half a mile of where they were born.

Bird migration, though predictable, is little understood and continues to puzzle scientists.

Depending on where you live, you should be able to observe bird migrations. Keep track of migration activity in early spring and again in early autumn. The best time of the day to do your observing is in the early morning.

In spring, make a list of the permanent residents, those birds that do not migrate. That way, you will be able to keep track of the migrants.

Visit different habitats such as forests, the shore, swamps, lakes, and fields. Remember that each bird has its own schedule and characteristic migration pattern. Your observations could take note of the following:

1. Do birds arrive at day or at night? Does the size of the bird have anything to do with arrival time?

2. Date of arrival and departure.

3. Do arriving or departing birds fly singly or in groups?

4. Are both sexes around at the same time in spring?

5. Can you find a flyway near you—a path that all incoming and outgoing birds seem to take? Use reference books to study maps of flyways.

6. Do any birds come to your area for the winter?

YOUR BEAK IS
WHAT YOU EAT

Is beak shape related to diet?

Observe birds eating seeds, worms, fish, rodents, and so on. Examine trees for signs of bird activity (for example, woodpeckers leave holes). Take careful notes on what you observe. How many beak shapes can you find and draw? What do you conclude?

ANIMAL BEHAVIOR

A valuable project is to study a wild animal in its natural habitat. Include in your observations its response to its own species, to other species, and to the nonliving environment. Pay attention to feeding, courtship, and defense of itself, its young, and its territory. Also note the way it communicates with other members of its species and with other species, as well as how it responds to external stimuli (wind, moisture, temperature, light).

Try to observe the animal without being seen. If possible, use binoculars or a field scope. If you can, take pictures or use a camcorder to record behavior. Take detailed notes in a field notebook.

PROBING OWL PELLETS

Owls and other birds of prey routinely regurgitate the undigested remains (bones, skin, feathers) of their prey. The study of these pellets is an interesting way to investigate the bird's diet and the distribution of the small mammals they eat.

You can buy owl pellets from biological supply companies, collect your own, or obtain them from zoos or aviaries. To collect your own, you will need to locate a roost. A field guide or bird behavior book will help you. Two tips are to listen for owls calling at night or very early in the morning and to look for "whitewash" (owl droppings) on trees in likely habitat areas.

If you are using fresh pellets, allow them to dry for several days. Dry pellets will easily crumble when you use a needle to separate out bones from pieces of skin and hair. Soak bones or feathers in household ammonia to remove any attached skin or soft tissues. Soak bones in household bleach to remove stains. **NEVER MIX AMMONIA AND BLEACH.**

CAREFUL! AVOID GETTING THESE CHEMICALS ON YOUR SKIN OR IN YOUR EYES.

Use field guides or the specific references given at the end of this chapter to identify bones. You may wish to draw the bones, too. Mammalian hairs can be identified using Wiliamson's *Aids to the Identification of Mole and Shrew Hairs,* available at any college library. Here are some questions to answer:

- What kind of owl has made the pellets you have?
- What is the owl's main diet?
- Do owls eat animals only?
- What other animals produce similar pellets?

FISH BEHAVIOR

Many interesting projects can be done with fish. You can obtain many fish from aquarium shops. Fish can also be observed in streams, lakes, and the ocean.

Schooling

A school of fish is a leaderless and close-knit group moving at the same pace and engaging in the same activity.

- Fill two 1-quart mayonnaise jars half full of water from a 10-gallon aquarium. Add 12 neon tetras to one jar and one tetra to the other jar. Add water to the top and seal with the lids. Place the jars, inverted, in the aquarium at opposite ends.

Introduce a single neon tetra into the middle of the aquarium. What happens? Repeat this part of the experiment by changing the number of fish in the jars. Do neons school? Experiment with other fish.

Be sure to release fish from the jars after experimenting.

- If you are near a river, lake, or tide pool, can you observe any schools of fish? Sometimes huge schools of fish (for example, anchovies, bluefish, and salmon) can be seen in rivers and the ocean. Investigate massive runs of fish like these.

• Can you affect schooling behavior with different types of lighting, with magnetic fields, sound waves, music, different-colored water, and so on?

Aggression
African ciclids and bettas, familiar in aquarium shops, are fish that display aggressive behavior. Devise experiments that show aggressive behavior (for example, raised gill covers, tail beating, fin spreading) among the same and opposite sex of these species when placed in individual, transparent containers set next to each other.

Investigate the effects on aggressive behavior of temperature, colors, drawings or models, light, outside movement, and so on. Do these fish react to seeing themselves in a mirror? If they do, how much of their image must they see to react?

Learning
How do fish locate their food? You can find out whether they use color by trying the following experiment.

Keep a single goldfish alone in an aquarium. Obtain or make three disks (using any waterproof material, for example, tiddlywinks), each ½–1 inch (1–3 cm) in diameter, of three different colors. Glue each disk to a stick or wire.

Drape tubifex red worms around one of the colored disks and immerse all three disks simultaneously in the water to the same depth.

Repeat this procedure three times a day for two to three days, always placing the food around the same color disk. On the fourth day, introduce the colored disks without food.

What happens? Why? Experiment with different colors of disks. If the fish seem to respond to color, how do you know they just aren't responding to the location of the food?

• Can you train fish to locate food in other ways, through lures or scents?

Light and Reproduction
Find out whether high-intensity white light affects reproduction in guppies. Does it affect courtship, fertility, egg development, egg-laying ability, and so on?

Temperature and Behavior
Use goldfish or guppies to study the effects of temperature on fish. The best way to change the temperature in an aquarium is to immerse plastic bags of hot or cold water into the water. Never exceed 85°F (30°C) or go below 55°F (14°C).

Does temperature affect general behavior, gill beating, courtship and reproduction (in guppies), or overall health?

In guppies, does temperature favor one sex over the other? Sex can be distinguished by comparing the distance between the anal and pelvic fins. This distance is longer in females than in males.

Environment and Growth
Does environment affect growth? Test the effects of crowding, quantity and quality of food, stimuli such as light and temperature, pH, air quality, sound, water movement, and magnetism on growth.

MUTUAL DEFENSE

There is safety in numbers. Animals often form groups to protect themselves from predators.

Investigate the phenomenon of flock defense. Construct a model of a predator (like a hawk) and rig it so that it will "fly" down a wire toward a bait site (scattered birdseed) that attracts many birds of the same species. If you can, use a movie camera or camcorder to record bird reactions—especially if the device has slow-motion capability. What flock size has the quickest reaction time to the model threat? Do the birds ever ATTACK the model?

DECOYS

Find out whether decoys like scarecrows and rooftop "owls" really work.

A TURTLE'S EAR
AND OTHER TALES

Can turtles hear? And if so, how?

First try to answer the first question. In your experiments, make sure you test all kinds of sounds, from whispering to bells, low sounds and very high sounds, loud and soft, and so on.

Find out whether the turtle uses its shell to help it hear.

When you're through experimenting with turtles, you may want to experiment with yourself or your friends, being careful not to risk damaging anyone's hearing by exposing them to sounds that are too loud or too high in frequency. Try the following activities with your ears plugged (use earplugs). Place a stick between your teeth and vibrate it. Can you hear it? Now vibrate it at arm's length. Can you hear anything now? Try the same using a rubber band. Hold the rubber band against the bone next to your ear on your cheek. Now vibrate the rubber band at arm's length.

What happens? Is this similar to the turtle's way of hearing?

Test the hearing of other animals.

A CLOSER LOOK
AT AMPHIBIANS

Amphibians generally live on land but return to the water to reproduce. Some familiar amphibians are frogs, toads, and salamanders. Amphibians are interesting vertebrates to study because of their ability to adapt to many environments.

Natural Population Control
Some animals seem to regulate the number of their young that mature. Find out whether this is the case with frogs.

Place one or two large tadpoles in a jar or aquarium with a group of much smaller tadpoles. Include a number of *Elodea* plants (available in pet shops) or pieces of lettuce as food. Over the next week, observe and record tadpole behavior.

Prepare another jar with small tadpoles, and into this jar pour the water from a jar containing much larger tadpoles. What happens? What do you think causes what you observed? Is it a chemical substance secreted by tadpoles themselves? Does diluting the water have any effect?

Consider the meaning of this effect in nature at times when food is scarce. Can you achieve the same effect in any other way or use other animals, like fish?

Camouflage
• *Melanocytes* are pigment cells in the skin of amphibians and other vertebrates. By contracting or expand-

ing, these cells can alter skin shade to help camouflage the animal. Observe different amphibians (for example, the leopard frog *Rana pipiens*, salamanders, toads, and newts) against backgrounds of different colors in zoos, pet shops, or the wild. Do a survey of which amphibians use camouflage, which are most successful, and whether they form different colors.

• Raise frog tadpoles to full size in tanks either by painting the outside of glass jars or small aquariums light or dark colors or by setting up one aquarium with lots of dark vegetation and another with minimal vegetation (only enough for food). Do the animals develop a different skin color in each rearing condition?

• Does temperature or light affect skin color?

Growth and Development
Study the effects of temperature, water quality, light, and other environmental factors on amphibian development. Collect egg masses (bunches of slimy strings or jelly masses) floating or attached to pieces of grass or twigs at the edges of ponds or other shallow waters. (They are also available from biological supply companies.) Place the egg masses in an aquarium to incubate and hatch tadpoles. Use a hand lens to observe individual eggs removed from the aquarium and placed in a shallow dish. Investigate the effect of low temperatures on egg development by using your refrigerator and comparing growth with similar eggs kept at room temperature in an aquarium.

Field Studies
In the spring, try to identify which amphibian breeds first by watching for egg masses. Use field guides to help identify amphibian egg masses.

Listen for amphibian mating calls. How far do they carry? Does one male's call affect other males? What time of day are frog calls most heard? Do weather conditions affect breeding behavior?

POPULATION CHANGES

Today, many naturalists use computer models to extend their powers of observation and simplify complex situations.

A simple computer population model is listed below. Type it into an Apple IIe or Apple IIgs computer and run the program. The program will ask you three questions: (1) What is the initial population?; (2) What growth rate will the population have?; (3) How many years do you want to monitor? The program will then graph the size of the population for each year. You must press Return to see the next year's data.

```
10 REM POPMODEL
20 TEXT : HOME
30 INPUT "WHAT IS THE STARTING POPULATION?:";PI
40 INPUT "THE PERCENT GROWTH RATE PER
     YEAR?:";PER
50 INPUT "HOW MANY YEARS?:";YEARS
60 GOSUB 1000
100 FOR I = 0 TO YEARS
110 VTAB 21 : HTAB 1 : PRINT "YEAR"; : HTAB 13 :
     PRINT "INITIAL POP"; : HTAB 26 : PRINT "CHANGE
     IN POP"
120 CHANGE = PI * PER / 100
130 VTAB 23 : HTAB 1 : PRINT I; : HTAB 13: PRINT INT
     (PI); : HTAB 26: PRINT INT (CHANGE);
135 PI = PI + CHANGE
140 IF I = 0 THEN HPLOT I * XSCAL,159 − PI * YSCAL
150 IF I < > 0 THEN HPLOT TO I * XSCAL,159 − PI *
     YSCAL
160 GET A$
170 NEXT I
```

```
190 END
1000 REM GRAPHING
1010 PG = PI
1020 FOR I = 0 TO YEARS
1030 PG = PG + PG * PER / 100
1040 NEXT I
1050 YSCAL = 158 / PG
1060 XSCAL = 279 / YEARS
1070 HGR : HCOLOR = 3
1080 HPLOT 0,0 TO 0,159 TO 279,159
1090 RETURN
```

Input various scenarios, varying each of the three parameters. For example, start with a small population that has a very low growth rate over a long time period. Then change each of the three parameters. What happens? Is the outcome always the same? You can use reference books to learn more about environmental and biological factors that limit populations. You can also contact your state conservation department to obtain actual data on population studies.

Read More About It

Arnosky, J. *Crinkleroot's Book of Animal Track and Wildlife Signs*. New York: Putnam, 1979.

Baker, A. A. *Field Photography: Beginning and Advanced Techniques*. San Francisco: Freeman, 1976.

Bell, C. *The Wonder of Snow*. New York: Hill and Wang, 1957

Conant, R. *A Field Guide to Reptiles and Amphibians*. Boston: Houghton Mifflin, 1975.

Gordon, M. *Guppies . . . As Pets*. Jersey City, N.J.: T.F.H. Publications, 1955.

Griffen, D. R. *Bird Migration*. New York: Natural History Press, 1964.

How to Prepare Skeletons. Rochester, N.Y.: Ward's Natural Science Establishment, 1962.

Mattison, C. *The Care of Reptiles and Amphibians in Captivity.* New York: Sterling, 1982.

Meyerriecks, A. J. *Courtship in Animals.* BSCS Pamphlet No. 3, Educational Programs Improvement Corp. Colorado Springs, Colo.: Colorado College, 1962.

Peterson, R. T. *Birds* (Peterson First Guides.) Boston: Houghton Mifflin, 1986.

Stokes, D. W. *A Guide to Nature in Winter.* Boston: Little, Brown, 1976.

Zappler, G., and L. Zappler. *Amphibians as Pets.* New York: Doubleday, 1973.

Zim, H., and H. Smith. *Reptiles and Amphibians.* New York: Golden Press, 1987.

8

NATURE
AT LARGE

All organisms on earth occupy small niches where they interact with other organisms and with the environment. All organisms are also part of a greater system—the biosphere—the fragile shell within which all life exists. For example, the fly buzzing inside your window is not only part of the local habitat, which includes you, your dog, the garbage out back, and the lawn in front. It is also part of the biosphere, which includes the oceans, atmosphere, mountains, weather systems, and all life-forms everywhere.

In recent years, the biosphere has come under increasing attack from the effects and by-products of civilization. Threats have included degradation of the ozone layer, acid rain, toxic waste and pesticides, soil erosion, and radiation. Looming above all these threats, of course, is the threat of nuclear war. Today we are beginning to deal with these challenges to the biosphere both in the scientific community and in the courts.

In this chapter, you will find projects that focus on the interrelationships between organisms and their environment.

NATURE'S FORGOTTEN RESOURCE—SOIL

Soil is composed of inorganic minerals, organic matter, living organisms, water, and gases, combined in a delicate balance. Soil sustains the crops that feed us and the trees that shelter us. Without soil, there would be few if any animals.

Because soil seems to exist in limitless quantities, we take it for granted. Yet each year, in the United States alone, six billion tons of soil is lost to the forces of erosion. If all this soil were collected on a 1-acre lot, the pile would be over 500 miles (800 km) high! Our soil is therefore a natural resource whose true value is often forgotten.

Erosion is caused by both natural forces and through the practices of human beings. To investigate the latter, you may wish to try the following project:

Line four shoe boxes with plastic sheeting. Cut a V-shaped notch in each box as a spout. Fill box 1 with firmly packed moist soil, box 2 with sod, box 3 with moist soil packed firmly with furrows running crosswise, and box 4 with three strips of moist packed soil alternated with three strips of sod. Position the boxes on supports so that they are all on the same incline. Place buckets under the spouts to collect the water and sediment runoff. Use a coffee can or an old bucket punched with small holes, or a sprinkling can to simulate rain.

Sprinkle water steadily for about 5 seconds onto each box. Record the amount of time the water continues to flow from the spout of each box. After the water has run off, measure the amount of sediment collected in the bucket.

Which land practice is best for preventing erosion? Which type of soil seems best? Can you devise some methods of combating erosion?

If possible, visit some local areas that suffer from erosion, either natural or man-made. Prepare a plan to repair the damage and prevent further loss of soil. You may want to use a camera or camcorder for this work. If you have a yard and your parents give you permission, see if you can overcome the forces of soil erosion. Be sure to document your work.

OTHER KINDS
OF EROSION

Investigate other kinds of erosion in nature. For example, there is erosion caused by wind and by the ocean. Rocks, though much harder than soil, are also eroded. Study stream bed erosion.

DESIGNING A
CLOSED ECOSYSTEM

In several places in the United States, and also in other countries, scientists are designing and testing environments called *closed ecosystems* to help them understand the problems that must be overcome if humans are ever to live for any extended time on the moon or on one of the planets.

In a closed ecosystem, no molecules can enter or leave; everything recycles: water, gases, nutrients, waste products, and life-forms.

Many popular magazine articles have been written about the Biosphere II project (the earth is Biosphere I) slated to begin in 1989. In *Cosmos*, Carl Sagan writes of the future of these enclosed systems being constructed to transport us to interstellar locations. Since 1977, NASA has been exploring closed ecosystems with its Controlled Ecological Life-Support System (CELSS) program.

Although you probably will not be able to seal in *every* molecule, you can experiment with closed ecosystems. They can be as large or as small as you want. To get started, use a large, wide-mouthed glass jar to enclose your pond ecosystem. The long-term success of your system depends on what life-forms you select. For the system to work properly (remain balanced), you will have to experiment to obtain the right mix of producers (plants), consumers (animals that eat other animals or plants), and decomposers (dependent upon dead and decaying plants and animals).

First add gravel to the jar to a depth of about 2 inches (5 cm). Slowly add water to fill the jar half full. Plant rooted plants in gravel; place others (like a banana plant) on top of the gravel. Let the water clear overnight. The next day, add snails, fish, and floating plants. Add more water to fill the jar to within 2 inches (5 cm) of the top. Use clear plastic wrap to cover the jar opening. Seal tightly by using rubber bands.

Place your system in indirect or dim light conditions. Position a 60- or 75-watt incandescent bulb about 8 inches (20 cm) from the top of the jar. Connect the light to a timer set to turn on the light for 16 hours each day.

Once you seal and position your system, watch it carefully. For example, the water may turn very green, signaling an imbalance. You may have to adjust the height of the light source or use a lower wattage light bulb. Look for other inbalances in your system and try to correct them. Can you map out the various relationships among producers, consumers, and decomposers?

You may want to set up other closed systems, like a terrestrial system containing mosses and lichens.

Once you have a "stable" system (usually in about a month), you can use it to investigate further.

Spring Flooding

In spring, heavy rains and heavy runoff from melting snow can carry high concentrations of nutrients from the soil into streams, rivers, and lakes, affecting the existing ecosystem. Design experiments to mimic these effects in your closed system. If you wish to work on the "real thing," be sure to do so under supervision of a qualified adult.

Microlife

Periodically sample your system and do some studies of these life-forms.

Environmental Health

Test the effects of temperature, color of light, pH, nutrient enrichment (pollution), and amount and intensity of light on your system. Can you observe or predict similar effects in the field?

Try to simulate the environmental effects that might be found on the moon, on a planet such as Mars, or on a moon such as Saturn's Titan. For example, the temperature range on the moon is much more extreme than on earth.

The Oxygen Cycle

You know that plants produce oxygen during photosynthesis. Since you have plants in your system, they should therefore be producing oxygen when they are photosynthesizing. Investigate oxygen production in your aquatic plants.

Would aquatic plants be a good source of oxygen in a closed ecosystem on, say, Mars? Would trees or other nonaquatic plants be better? Could plants be counted on as the only oxygen source for humans and other animals? What about other life-forms—protists, bacteria? What and where is the main source of oxygen on earth?

BIOMES

A biome is a region with a characteristic plant cover and life-forms. For example, tundra is a biome. It is arctic land with permanently frozen subsoil and low-growing plants. Only the soil surface thaws in the summer. This biome encircles the earth only in the northern latitudes. Can you explain why?

Each biome is characterized by its stable vegetation, called *climax vegetation*. Human intervention or a natural disaster (insect infestation, fire, hurricane, flood, and so on) can remove the vegetation, but over time the climax vegetation will reappear if the region is left undisturbed. This restoration process is called *succession*.

The two major biomes in the United States are grassland and temperate deciduous forest. Figure 28 illustrates the major biomes.

Identify the biome you live in, or any other nearby. Locate a healthy community (section) of one of these biomes, one minimally affected by human activity. Make an inventory of all the living things you observe in the five kingdoms. Construct a food web for this community. (A food web is a food scheme of overlapping and interlinking food chains used to complete a picture of "who eats what." A food chain is a food relationship beginning with a producer, eaten by a consumer, in turn eaten by another consumer, and so on.) Take careful notes on environmental factors such as amount of light, temperature, and precipitation. Note seasonal changes. If possible, study adjacent biomes.

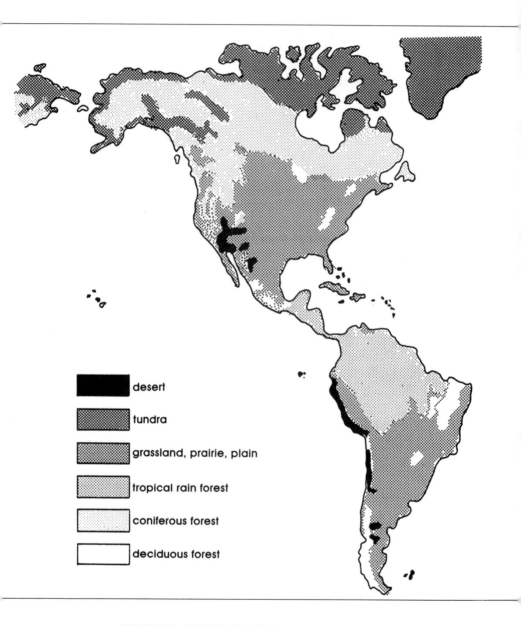

	desert
	tundra
	grassland, prairie, plain
	tropical rain forest
	coniferous forest
	deciduous forest

FIGURE 28. BIOMES OF NORTH AND SOUTH AMERICA

Do the biomes fade into each other, or is there a sharp break between them? If there is a sharp break, do you observe anything special on the "line"? Do the characteristics you note for the biome or biomes match those they are supposed to have? Explain any differences.

Use weather data to construct a climatogram (temperature plotted against rainfall) for the biome(s). Compare your data with data published for biomes. Can you draw any conclusions about the significance of weather in defining a biome?

A Study in Succession
The eruption of Mount St. Helens in 1980 destroyed part of the coniferous biome, leaving the region looking like a moonscape. Given enough time (perhaps a thousand years), the region will return to a climax community of conifers.

You can observe succession on a smaller time scale. Succession takes place in gradual stages, each with its own particular vegetation type, all the way to stable (climax) vegetation characterizing the biome. Begin by observing "bare earth" (recently cleared land) or clear a small lot (after obtaining permission) in a particular community of the biome you live in. Observe which life-forms (weeds, lichens, insects) first appear. Take notes, make drawings, and take photographs of the area throughout the observation period. To speed things up, try to find other areas that were once cleared (a couple of years previously) and observe which plants are now in evidence. Has the animal life changed as well? In comparing these different locations at various stages of succession, do you observe differences in certain plant and animal populations between study areas? Make a chart that lists the changes and illustrate it with photographs.

SOIL ACIDITY
AND SALINITY

Different soils, as you know, often contain different amounts of certain chemicals, including acids and salts.

• Find out whether soil acidity affects plant growth. Do some plants prefer an acid soil? An alkaline soil?

Experiment in the lab with different plants and types of soil. Regulate the acidity or alkalinity of some soils yourself. You can also work in the field. In some areas, for example, you may find stunted conifers, or no maples, or barren fields. Use a soil test kit or pH paper in your investigations.

• Find out whether moss growth is an indication of acid soil. If so, try to use moss growth in place of a soil test kit or pH paper in your field studies.

• Study the effects of salinity on plant growth. If you live near the ocean, see if salinity affects nearby plant growth and types. Also study farmers' fields irrigated with ground water.

ACID RAIN

In recent years, a new threat to our environment has arisen: acid rain. Although all rain is acidic, some rain is so acidic that it can damage lakes and rivers, killing fish, plants, and other life. Acid rain is so acidic because it contains the acidic by-product of fossil fuel combustion emitted by cars but mostly by factories.

Natural rainwater is slightly acidic and has a pH of 5.6. pH is a measure of acidity, with 7 being neither acid nor base and lower numbers representing increasingly higher acidity. The average rainstorm in the eastern United States produces rain with a pH of 4.2, *twenty-five* times more acidic than ordinary rainwater. Acid rain is defined as any rain with a pH below 5.6. Since most organisms live within a narrow range of pH in the environment, a pH shift of one or two pH units can kill many organisms, or wipe out entire biological communities.

You can investigate acidity in the field or in the laboratory, using strips of Universal pH paper which measure the entire 1–14 pH scale, available from biological supply companies.

• Gather together an assortment of solutions to measure tap water, distilled water, orange juice, lemon juice, soda pop, bleach, baking soda dissolved in water, and so on. Chart your solution measurements (in pH units) on a chart. Use the chart for later comparisons with observations in the field. For example, is rainwater more or less acidic than vinegar?

• Collect and test the pH of rainwater gathered in cleaned containers at various times during a rainstorm or a snowstorm. Collect water samples from lakes, ponds, rivers, and puddles.

• Tiny aquatic animals such as plankton vary in their sensitivity to acid in their habitats. You can collect plankton using a homemade plankton tow net made from an old nylon stocking, as shown in Figure 29.

Cut the toe from the stocking. Make a ring 8 inches (20 cm) in diameter from a coat hanger and attach the wide end of the stocking to the ring. Attach a glass vial to the narrow end of the stocking.

To collect specimens, attach a tow line (made from fishing line) to the large end of the stocking and drag it while walking along the shore or a dock or while riding in a slow-moving boat. The stocking will strain out larger organisms, allowing plankton to slip through and collect in the vial.

Capture as many tiny organisms as possible, divide them into two batches, and add them with equal amounts of pond water to two glass containers. Mea-

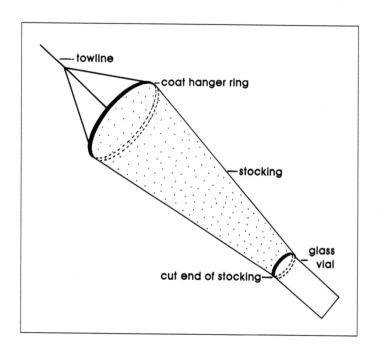

FIGURE 29. MAKING A PLANKTON TOW NET

sure the acidity of the water. Keep one container as a control and alter the acidity of the other by adding very small amounts of vinegar or lemon juice over time. Try to identify the organisms. Study your two environments closely over a couple of days—longer if possible.

Determine the effects, if any, of the increased acidity. Which organisms, if any, are most acid resistant over time? At the conclusion of your study, which environment has the most diverse animal population?

• Can you think of a solution to the acid rain crisis facing Canada, the United States, and other countries?

MILKWEED

The perennial wildflower milkweed can be seen as patches of pinkish-purple colorings along roadsides, fields, and meadows throughout North America. The plant gets its name from the thick, milky white latex it produces for defense against predators, and serves as a unique stage for observing ecological interrelationships.

Observe milkweed plants closely over several days and at night. Cover a flashlight with red cellophane to allow you to observe insects without disturbing them. Try to identify as many creatures as you can. Try to assign occupations (who eats whom) to the animals observed. Knowing what each organism does will help you construct a relationship diagram (a food web) for the milkweed plant community (the populations of organisms that live and interact in the same place). You should have no trouble identifying at least ten different species. Prepare a diagram, or possibly a dried collection of various residents and visitors to the plant.

Read More About It

Acid Rain: What It Is—How You Can Help!. National Wildlife Federation, 1412 16th St. NW, Washington, D.C. 20036. (Single copies free.)

The Acid Rain Story. Information Directorate, Environment Canada, Ottawa, Ontario, K1A 0H3.

Brady, N. C. *The Nature and Property of Soils.* 8th ed. New York: Macmillan, 1974.

Croall, S., and W. Ranklin. *Ecology For Beginners.* New York: Random House, 1982.

Garber, S. *The Urban Naturalist.* New York: Wiley, 1986.

Karstad, A. *Alet Karstad's Canadian Nature Notebook.* Toronto: McGraw-Hill Ryerson, 1979.

Lincoln, R., and G. Boxshall. *The Cambridge Illustrated Dictionary of Natural History.* New York: Cambridge University Press, 1987.

Margulis, Lynn, and Dorion Sagan. *Micro-cosmos.* New York: Summit Books, 1986.

Morse, D. H. "Milkweeds and Their Visitors." *Scientific American.* 253:112–119, 1985.

Palmer, E. L. (rev. by) H. S. Fowler. *Fieldbook of Natural History,* 2nd ed. New York: McGraw-Hill, 1975.

Red Herring: Myths and Facts about Acid Rain. The Izaak Walton League of America, 1800 N. Kent St., Suite 806, Arlington, Va. 22209. (Free)

Sagan, Carl. *Cosmos.* New York: Random House, 1980.

Taub, F. B. "Closed Ecological Systems." *Annual Review of Ecology and Systematics.* 5:139–160, 1974.

An Updated Perspective on Acid Rain. Edison Electric Institute, 1111 19th St. NW, Washington, D.C. 20036. (Free)

APPENDIX
SOURCES OF MATERIALS

Much of the material and equipment a naturalist needs can be obtained from around the house, or from the local pharmacy or hardware store.

However, if you wish to expand your home laboratory or obtain a hard-to-find life-form, the following firms offer a complete line of science material, including those referred to in this book.

Most supply companies will supply material if an order is accompanied by a check. One company (Edmund) will provide a catalog if you call; ask to borrow your teacher's catalogs for information about other companies.

American Biological Supply Company
1330 Dillon Heights Avenue
Baltimore, MD 21228
(301) 747-1797
(Equipment and apparatus only)

Carolina Biological Supply Company
2700 York Road
Burlington, NC 27215
(800) 547-1733

Connecticut Valley Biological Supply Company
82 Valley Road
South Hampton, MA 01073

Edmund Scientific
101 E. Glouster Pike
Barrington, NJ 08008
(609) 573-6250
(Equipment and apparatus only)

Science Kit and Boreal Laboratories
777 East Park Drive
Tonawanda, NY 14150
(800) 828-7777

Ward's Natural Science Establishment
5100 West Henrietta Road
P.O. Box 92912
Rochester, NY 14692-9012
(800) 962-2660

INDEX

Nitrogen, and bacteria, 26

Nitrogen cycle, *39*

Oxygen, and bacteria, 26; by-product of photosynthesis, 35, 65; cycle, 126–127; and magnetotactic bacteria, 42

Pasteur, Louis, 12
Pasteurization, 33
Penicillin, *47*
Pesticides, 30, 85, 95
pH, 48, 79, 126, 130–131
Pheromones, 98
Photosynthesis, 35–36, 64–66, 71, 79, 87. *See also* Chlorophyll
Pitfall traps, *97*–98
Planaria, 91
Plankton, 131–*132*
Plant presses, 66–69, *67*
Plants, 12, 64–87; buds, 70; cacti, 66, 87; capillary action, 75; carnations, 70; carnivorous, 83, 84, 90; clover, 38–40; as dyes, 80; ferns, 66, 85; field guides, 66, 69, 70; flowers, 65, 70–71; fruit, 85; gymnosperms, 85; habitat diary, 66; habitats, 72; initial colonizers, 69; leaf impressions, 86–87;

leaves, 65, *68*, 71, 80–81; leguminous, 40; and magnetic fields, 42; maladies, 69; pigment separation, *78*; pitcher plants, 84; rhododendrons as thermometers, 80; root observation box, *83*; roots, 30, 66, 69–70, 72–73, 83–84; seeds, 85–86; soil acidity, 130; stalks, 70; stems, 66, 70–71; sundew, 84; as thermometers, 80; tube bundles, 70; venus flytrap plants, 83, 84, 90; vines, 83; weather forecasting, 71; xylem, 70. *See also* Trees
"Point source" of illumination, 18
Pollinators, 73
Pollution, 36, 53, 97
Population, computer model, 119–120
Protists, 12, 15, 25, 55–62; cysts, 60, 61; feeding strategies, 60; freshwater, *56*; identification guides, 60; insect, *62*; lichens, 51–53; and magnetic fields, 42; and oxygen, 127; *paramecium*, 15; sensitivities to stimuli, 60–61; *volvox*, 15

Protozoa, 12, 55

Recycling, chemical components of life, 26
Replica impressions, 30
Rotifers, 91

Safety precautions, 22–24, 26, 30, 31, 33; acetone, 77; antibacterial agent testing, 38; chemical use, 112–113; for handling animal gut contents, 61; iodine dyes, 65; mushrooms, eating of, 44; spider collecting, 99
Sagan, Carl, 124–125
Science, 14
Scientific method, 11–13
Sea anemones, 89
Seaweeds, 55, 58–60, *59*
Seeds, gravity effect, *82*
Septic tank products, and bacteria, 33
Serendipity, 12
Sheet metal, 34
Shellfish, 92–93
Sink factor, 107–110, *109*
Skeletons, 106–107
Slugs, 85, 91–94
Snails, 92–94
Snowshoe hares, 108–110, *109*
Soil, 123–124; acidity, 130; bacteria, 60; salinity, 130; test kits, 48, 130

Solvent front, 77, 79
Species, 12
Stains. *See* Dyes
Starch, 65, 69
Starch tests, 69
Sugaring, 99
Swarmer cells, 61
Systema Naturae, 12

Trees, growth rings, *74–75*. *See also* Plants
Tropisms, 81–84; gravitropisms, 81–83; haptotropisms, 81; hydrotropisms, 81, 83–84; phototropisms, 81
Turtles, way of hearing, 116–117
Tyndall, John, 32
Tyndall effect, 32–33
Tyndallization, 33

Variables, 14
Vertebrates, 106–121
Visual Guide to Fungi Types, 46, 49–50

Water fleas, *23*
Weather forecasting, using plants, 71
Weed control, without chemicals, 73
Wet mounts, 19, 22, *68*; of gut contents, 61; making of, *62*; of protists, 61; of wild fungus, 44–45
Worms, 94–95

ABOUT THE AUTHOR

Kenneth Rainis is a professional biologist who works for a well-known biological supply company. He graduated from Quincy College in 1973 with a BSc in biology. In 1976, he received a Master's degree in zoology from Iowa State University. Mr. Rainis is the author of many articles and products for science education and is a contributor to the textbook *Biological Science: an Ecological Approach.* For over fifteen years, he has judged both regional and state-level science fairs. This is his first book.